# Praise for *Face It*

*"A smart book for smart women. There is something here for all of us, and it is a perfect gift for others we care about."*
— **Hoda Kotb**, co-host, the *Today* show

*"Finally, not just another beauty book. As someone in the public eye, I truly appreciate the authors' understanding— having been there themselves—of how all women deal with complicated reactions to their aging appearance. Face It offers a refreshing perspective and long-lasting solutions. It's a book you can give to your mother, your daughter, or any woman who wants to feel and look great at any age."*
— **Sela Ward**, actress

*"Face It is the thinking woman's guide to looking and being one's best at any age. Tapping into 'the closet fears' of every woman's vanity, the authors provide well-researched, healthy initiatives for a generation of readers caught in the conflict of chasing waning youth versus aging with grace, confidence, and innovation."*
— **Andrea Robinson**, former beauty editor of *Vogue;* former president of Ultima 11, Ralph Lauren Fragrances, Tom Ford Beauty, and Prescriptives

*"This book is a wakeup call to the beauty industry . . . as it deals with the true core of women's feelings as they age. It makes you realize that yet another 'anti-aging' cream or procedure is not the panacea. It is the definition of beauty that needs to evolve as we age, to be broader, more realistic, and accepting than the narrow, physical definition that is ingrained in our psyches."*
— **Daria Myers**, co-founder and former president, Origins

# face it

# face it

## What Women *Really* Feel
## as Their Looks Change

A Psychological Guide to Enjoying
Your Appearance at Any Age

VIVIAN DILLER, Ph.D.,

with Jill Muir-Sukenick, Ph.D.

Edited by Michele Willens

**HAY HOUSE, INC.**
Carlsbad, California • New York City
London • Sydney • Johannesburg
Vancouver • Hong Kong • New Delhi

**Published and distributed in the United States by:** Hay House, Inc.: www.hayhouse.com • **Published and distributed in Australia by:** Hay House Australia Pty. Ltd.: www.hayhouse.com.au • **Published and distributed in the United Kingdom by:** Hay House UK, Ltd.: www.hayhouse.co.uk • **Published and distributed in the Republic of South Africa by:** Hay House SA (Pty), Ltd.: www.hayhouse.co.za • **Distributed in Canada by:** Raincoast: www.raincoast.com • **Published in India by:** Hay House Publishers India: www.hayhouse.co.in

*Design:* Jen Kennedy

Library of Congress Cataloging-in-Publication Data

Diller, Vivian.
  Face it : what women really feel as their looks change : a psychological guide to enjoying your appearance at any age / Vivian Diller with Jill Muir-Sukenick ; edited by Michele Willens.
    p. cm.
  Includes bibliographical references.
  ISBN 978-1-4019-2540-6 (hardcover : alk. paper) 1. Body image. 2. Feminine beauty (Aesthetics) 3. Self-esteem in women. 4. Older women. I. Muir-Sukenick, Jill, 1953- II. Willens, Michele, 1948- III. Title.
  BF697.5.B63D55 2010
  155.9'1--dc22                                        2009038608


ISBN: 978-1-4019-2540-6

13 12 11 10   4 3 2 1
1st edition, February 2010

Printed in the United States of America

To our families
and friends, who make
our lives beautiful.

. . .

# Contents

# preface

. . .

## A Unique Perspective:
## From Modeling to Psychotherapy

For 20 years, Dr. Sukenick and I have been interested in the psychology of beauty and the role it plays in women's lives. As former models, and now as therapists, we have had the unique opportunity to spend time immersed in two very different worlds: one in which physical appearance plays an all-important role and one where it is often relegated to irrelevant. We have interviewed hundreds of women from all walks of life and learned the following: *all* women, regardless of their backgrounds, have strong physical *and* emotional reactions to changes in their appearance as they age. In fact, these changes set in motion a complicated psychological process that prompts most women to reflect upon profound life questions like, *"Who am I?"* and, *"What is to become of me?"* It is this process that led us to write this book.

Dr. Sukenick and I first met in 1988. We were with our husbands, who had attended the same university, when they ran into each other at a coffee shop. We began talking, and it turned out we had a lot in common. We had both been models in the '70s: I was represented by the Wilhelmina agency at the same time Jill modeled with Ford. When our careers ended, we returned to school to get our Ph.D.s, got married, had children, and went on to do postdoctoral training in psychoanalysis. A friendship developed and an intellectual adventure did, too.

We spent the next decade building our practices and raising our families, but the origins of this book were born in that coffee shop.

We continued to reminisce about our modeling days, and their aftermath. We agreed there had been exciting aspects—meeting interesting people, traveling new places, seeing ourselves in print and on television. But there had also been stressful ones—backbiting competition, relentless scrutiny, and the constant anticipation of aging out of our careers. We began to wonder what had become of some of our fellow models as they also left that world. We were struck by how many ended up feeling washed up, drifted in and out of relationships, and had problems with drugs or alcohol. Women who once had so much—beauty, access to money, and adoration—seemed to end up with so little.

It got us thinking. Why had we been able to make the transition, albeit a difficult one, from a profession so focused on almost *un*real beauty, to one in which our looks were not our primary asset? Were there identifiable themes that differentiated those who landed on their feet from those who didn't? We realized we had a unique vantage point from which to probe further. We had an opportunity to learn about the internal experience of women, in general, dealing with how they look, particularly as they age. Most important, we had the ability to help make it a less confusing and frightening experience.

We conducted in-depth interviews with women between ages 35 and 65. We also gathered data from a survey on self-esteem and beauty that we created for a national magazine. We used the results from both to help determine the factors that contributed to a successful shift from lives focused on beauty to lives where it played a far lesser role. The data confirmed our belief that to some degree, all women connect their self-worth to how they look. Most interesting was the finding that there were parallels between the emotional turmoil models suffered as their careers faded and the experience of everyday women as they aged. The runways may be different, but the issues and emotions are much the same.

As we discussed our data with others, we realized we were touching upon an issue on the minds of many women, especially those reaching midlife. It is complicated by the fact that we are part of a generation brought up with paradoxical messages about beauty—it matters, it doesn't; it should, it shouldn't. We were raised to believe we could rely on our education, money, and talent to control our futures. Yet we now feel out of control over the changes we see in the mirror: the creeping gray hair, yellow teeth, brown spots—pick from your palette. This book is our attempt to help women regain a sense of control by being as smart about appearance as we are about other aspects of our busy and fulfilling lives.

What this book is not, is a laundry list of how to's and how not to's. There are no simple solutions to the complex emotions women feel as their looks change. Instead, we carefully break down this highly charged emotional experience into psychological steps to make it less confusing and more manageable. Aging has no exact beginning or end, like a divorce, an illness, or a troublesome issue at work. We do not claim to have "been there, done that." The challenges of aging are ongoing and require solutions that evolve and change as we do. Our goal—as psychologists who were once models—is to alter the way women approach their changing looks so they can view themselves from new perspectives. In the end, we hope the phrase "looking as good as you feel" goes from being a pleasant-sounding cliché to a genuine way of life.

Let's face it: women are understandably perplexed as their appearance changes. But contrary to the cultural messages surrounding us, we neither need to return to youthful looks, nor dismiss them entirely, to enjoy our aging bodies and faces. Rather we need to embrace the multidimensional meaning of beauty that begins with Webster's dictionary definition—"a quality that gives pleasure or exalts the mind"—and go deeper beneath and ultimately beyond.

— Vivian Diller, Ph.D.

# introduction

• • •

## To Care or Not to Care about Beauty?

*Among the beliefs I held about the world
was that being beautiful should not matter to a
woman because it was one of those things that would
go away . . . and there wouldn't be anything
you could do to bring it back.*

— Jamaica Kincaid

## That Is Our Question

Marlene is 57 and by all accounts successful: she is a wife, a mother of two, and a top salesperson in a major department store. She takes great pride in being able to balance time with her family with the demands at work. Yet lately the only "work" on her mind has been what she wants to do to her face. Something, anything!

And then there's the ambivalence and guilt. She says, *"I know it goes against everything women of my generation should care about, but I just don't like what I see . . . my sagging skin, puffiness around my eyes. I'm bothered by the idea that if I don't do something—or even if I do—it might affect my career. I want to be true to who I am inside, but I also want to look as good as I feel. I am not a superficial person so it amazes me that I am having such a hard time getting older and looking my age. I feel so many mixed emotions."*

Let's face it: this is a journey Marlene—and most of us—never expected to be taking. We may be reading about marriage, mothering, and even menopause, but a book about aging looks? Sure, some women sneak a peek at an infomercial and others find a spare hour for a facial or a waxing. But do any of us really want to spend more time going deeper underneath those surfaces? We have worked too hard and long to ensure our lives would be governed by equality and choice simply to end up feeling trapped by such superficial concerns. In any case, weren't our physical features supposed to take care of themselves?

Well, as F. Scott Fitzgerald wrote, *"wouldn't it be pretty to think so?"*

The truth is, millions of us now in our 40s, 50s, and 60s are preoccupied with thinking about the physical realities that come with growing older. We anxiously stare into our mirrors like insecure adolescents and are surprised, and *embarrassed,* that we care so much. We reject the idea of being solely the object of desire and fantasy, yet who among us does not want to be regarded as attractive? We try seeking comfort from the age-old adage "beauty is in the eye of the beholder," but modern reality tells us *not* to age, that good looks are our currency, our power, and what makes us vital in today's world.

These conflicting messages are coming at us not only from magazines, movies, blogs, and tweets, but from our equally confounded contemporaries. We are not sure what to make of our smart, savvy friends who flaunt their feminism only to appear suddenly and mysteriously rested? We condemn 17-year-old wannabes trying to look 30, yet we condone 60-year-olds trying to look 40. Is this blatant hypocrisy? Or is this a reflection of an ambivalent and confused generation of women?

Sometimes the mixed messages come from our own loved ones, who give a year's supply of Botox on Mother's Day or suggest liposuction as a Valentine's gift. We may joke about it, as Carrie Fisher did on national television when she admitted, *"my mother offered to buy me a face-lift for Christmas!"* But the joke is on us when the cards attached to these alleged self-improvement gifts tell us we are loved for who we are! Surely they know aging is the gift that keeps on giving.

More than ever before, women are turning to quick fixes and cosmetic surgery to "solve" the bewilderment they see in their faces. Some of us are appalled that we have come *this* far yet are willing to go *that* far trying not to look old. Many have decided that dream creams and injected faces are more politically palatable than surgically tightened and lifted ones. Most of us seem flummoxed as we try to avoid coming in last in a race we didn't expect to run.

Making matters worse is that, all too often, this battle is waged secretly, within our own minds and in isolation. Although we openly share our troubles about work, relationships, and children, we tend to keep concerns about our changing looks hidden from others. We worry as we witness wandering husbands, or peers passed over by younger colleagues, but we don't dare expose our anxieties over what we suspect provoked these events. *"Who, me? Concerned about wrinkles?"* Ask yourself: Have you told even your closest friends about your injections? Have they told you about theirs?

As modern women, we have valiantly stayed the course forged by feminism, appreciative of the path our predecessors paved. Yet when faced with our changing appearance, we find ourselves pulled in opposite directions, stuck in a paradox and bound for failure. Remember, we are the generation of women who subscribed to society's unrealistic recipe for success: the ambitious professional, loyal wife, *and* competent mother. For decades we have come to expect—and are expected—to have it all and to do it all. The attempt alone is worth a medal, especially since we aspire to show little wear and tear for all our juggling and multitasking. This much is clear: we are buying—and buying *into*—an anxiety-producing cultural imperative to look younger than we truly are. And we are terribly uncomfortable as we succumb to the siege of internal and external pressures tugging at us from so many directions.

Comedian Tina Fey addressed the dilemma facing today's women: *"'You can have it all and be serious,' but also, 'It's great to get Botox,' and 'You should be really skinny but don't be, but don't not be!'"* Surely it helps to laugh, but we need to bring these mixed messages into a more serious discussion to find a resolution. Otherwise we render ourselves more vulnerable to a culture that has us paralyzed by what we call the beauty paradox.

## Paradox Need Not Lead to Paralysis

The beauty paradox is the predicament created by two incompatible messages that our generation has internalized. To navigate through this cultural quagmire, we first need to clarify the conflicting messages.

. . .

*Message 1: Deny.* **Your looks shouldn't matter. If they do, don't let anyone know. Stay true to your real self. Let your looks take their natural course as you age.**

*Message 2: Defy.* **Your looks should matter, and don't you ever forget that. Buy wrinkle creams, work out at the gym, and defy aging at whatever the cost, in any way you can. Oh, and be sure to make it look natural!**

. . .

These contradictory messages present an obstacle course in the path women take toward feeling and looking good as they age. As therapists, we see an increasing use of maneuvers to avoid the pitfalls that stand in the way of reaching that goal. Some are extreme, like excessive dieting, alcohol or drug use, and repeated plastic surgery. Others are less radical, like age-defying cosmetics, new wardrobes, and young boyfriends. Some are mental maneuvers, less clear and less tangible—*"this is not my issue,"* or *"who, me?"* Women try to get out of the race—*"I can't win this one."* And, some are stuck, immobilized by opposing forces—*"dare I care—dare I not?"* Still others equivocate, going back and forth seeking different methods to relieve their ambivalence.

*Face It* provides a road map to resolve this beauty paradox. You will be guided through six psychological steps that were specifically designed to help women change the way they feel about their looks as they age. This process has been proven to be effective in our clinical practices, using a method that moves from the external to the internal, from the surface to deep within. You will find no quick fixes here. No nips and tucks except to your attitudes and emotions. Nor will you be left with lofty ideas about ageless beauty without the means to emotionally and physically achieve it. This six-step process is realistic yet not simplistic. The results are thorough and long lasting.

Our practices reveal what research confirms: women have lost their equilibrium and are eager to find a path that will steady them as they age. Our approach is unique in that it does not require choosing an extreme position—that beauty does or does not matter. The beauty paradox need not mean paralysis, nor should it provoke unnecessary panic. Our process moves women toward their goal carefully and thoughtfully. It is anchored by the belief that looks have value at any age and caring for them requires effort at every age. It is less about *whether* our appearance matters or not, and more about *how* we choose to care. Finding balance, satisfaction, and pleasure as your appearance changes with age is our objective.

•  •  •

**Although we might not be able to alter the current culture of beauty that surrounds us, we can change how we experience it and how we let it define us. If each one of us takes a more active stance toward redefining beauty on our own terms, we may ultimately have an impact on our culture and on the meaning beauty has for the next generation.**

## Finding our Balance One Step at a Time

We break down the process of change into six psychological steps. *Step One* describes women's experiences of "uh-oh" moments, the initial confrontations with our changing looks. These are moments of recognition, and the feelings provoked by them need to be acknowledged and dealt with appropriately. We know it's an emotional place you don't necessarily want to go, so *Step Two* helps you identify what we call "masks." These are the maneuvers we use to conceal our feelings from others and even ourselves. We clarify how these masks attempt to shield us from the impact of our aging appearance but in the end are ineffective. As you recognize that you are not alone and become less fearful about what lies behind your mask, you will more confidently face the mirror.

Next we go to *Step Three,* where we teach you how to listen to your internal dialogues. These dialogues are the words you hear inside your head that reflect the multilayered experience you have about your looks. Some of these internal conversations may have been there for many years. Some may be responses to the culture that surrounds you. These words and feelings may confuse you or you may not want to hear them, but you will begin to understand why it is so important to pay attention to them. We want you to listen to yourself with care and courage so that critical internal voices become supportive and self-respecting. The new tone of these voices will ultimately provide the confidence your self-image needs as you age.

To gain insight and move forward, you need to go backward. *Step Four* takes you back in time to examine how the significant people in your personal history contributed to the development of self-image. You will look at how your parents' actions or words, or lack of them, played a role in your sense of attractiveness. The focus will be on Mother, since she is the figure that is most often tied to your identity. We'll also encourage you to examine your relationships with your father, siblings, and other significant people, because they impact self-image as well.

We then go to *Step Five,* where we take you back to adolescence. It's a time many of us prefer to keep buried in old yearbooks, but we take you there because it parallels most closely the transitional stage of life you are in now. Adolescence and midlife are times when self-image and sexual identity undergo vast change. You will discover that you are probably having adolescent-like reactions to your current transitions, like moodiness, sensitivity to loss, even irrational jealously. While your teenage years may have been turbulent, they served to promote separation and growth. Your feelings at midlife can also be used productively, but this time around, we will show you how to handle yourself more calmly and maturely.

Once you understand the role your looks played in your past, we will help you take the final step and make the inevitable shift in self-image that comes with aging. In *Step Six,* you will learn that holding on, especially to youthful definitions of beauty, doesn't work. Just as we can't bring back a beloved relative who has passed away, we can't bring back the young girls we once were. You will understand that aging gracefully and beautifully has a lot to do with absorbing losses. Accepting that we have to let go of an essential aspect of who we are as women is the most difficult task for many of us. But we will show you how to mourn the loss of youthful looks in such a way that you are not left in despair or fearful of your future. In the end, you will permanently alter your perspective on the subject of beauty.

Mark Twain once wrote: *"Age is an issue of mind over matter. If you don't mind, it doesn't matter."* Well, for contemporary women, it's just not that simple. It is time to recognize that the disquieting emotions women feel about their changing looks are reflections of a deeper, more complex experience than what has traditionally and automatically been labeled as superficial vanity. We all need to accept the reality that our sense of well-being is at least partly invested in the face we present to the world. Our appearance matters in spite of, and perhaps even because of, all the advances that have led us to live long and productive lives.

Let's face it: looking and feeling great matters at every age, and it is time to bring this topic into the conversations among smart and thoughtful women.

# SECTION I

Setting the Stage
for Change

# chapter one

· · ·

## A Generation Lost and Confused

*The democratic idea has not extended to aesthetic
variation; instead the aesthetic idea has paradoxically
become narrower over the last few decades.*

— Susie Orbach

### Is This What We Fought For?

Beauty is antithetical to our democratic ideals. It is distributed unfairly and unequally and this does not sit well with other values held by most evolved women. Consequently, many of us deal with the subject of beauty by dismissing it as insufficiently weighty, anti-feminist, unintellectual, and culturally induced. Others hold contempt for those who are blessed with great genes. Some just cope by using cognitive dissonance, a mental trick that allows us to feel more comfortable with a reality we cannot control: concluding, for example, that most beautiful women are stupid. Sure, we've occasionally heard of the brainy blonde but not nearly as often as her dumb counterpart.

In spite of these cognitive acrobatics and rationalizations, so many of us continue to struggle reconciling who we are with how we look. Why does our appearance matter to us even if our politics, beliefs, and intellect tell us it shouldn't? To understand this dilemma, we have to recognize the biological and cultural roles beauty plays in our lives.

3

. . .

**What has always been true is that beauty, in its purest sense, is a universal staple of human experience. It plays a powerful and fundamental role in our personal and professional lives. It is a basic human pleasure that will never go away.**

. . .

Scientific studies have been conducted to demonstrate that humans are hardwired to react to beauty. Recent research supports the belief that attractive physical features serve evolution, propelling the survival of our species. Psychosociologists examining the psychology of beauty infer that people who are commonly considered attractive seem to survive better than those who aren't. This has led them to theorize that good-looking people may have stronger immune systems, more robust genes, and higher mate-value.[1] Other studies tell us that what is considered attractive is similar across varied and unrelated cultures; for example, men generally are more attracted to women with large eyes and small noses set in round faces—features often associated with infants.[2] And MRI and PET scans provide further evidence about the importance of beauty: Female brain activity has been shown to increase when women are told they are being admired by men. Male brains register more activity when viewing women they consider attractive.[3]

Developmental research reveals that newborns not only quickly recognize facial features but also demonstrate preference for faces independently rated as attractive.[4] This natural bias for beauty evolves into deep-seated stereotypes that result in a psychological phenomenon called "the Halo Effect," which says that the quality of one trait is automatically applied to all parts of the object being observed. For example, someone who is regarded as beautiful is also assumed to be responsible, intelligent, adaptable, and so on.[5] This translates into a tendency for attractive people to be hired faster, get better jobs, earn more money, and even get acquitted more often.[6] In essence, those who are physically blessed are not simply accorded more leeway in life, they are universally and positively recognized and rewarded.

It's not surprising then that the desire to be attractive and perceived as such remains important to women of all ages across the world and spans all ages. Sociologist Naomi Wolf writes, *"Beauty is a currency system like the gold standard."* Most women agree, reporting that good looks continue to be associated with respect, legitimacy, and power in their relationships with others. Actress and model Isabella Rossellini says, *"In monetary terms, beauty pays more than anything."*

What do these facts and inequities about physical beauty mean to a generation of women whose childlike faces are fast becoming distant memories? It could lead you to conclude that we are right back where we started, with science confirming the sentiment supported by so many popular books—that it is what's outside that counts and that we should, in fact, seek ways for *how not to look old.* Or, accept our biology and resign ourselves to an inevitable fate, as Lucille Ball jokingly suggested, *"The secret of staying younger is to live honestly, eat slowly, and lie about your age."* Easy to say, but it's not so simple.

To truly understand beauty is to view it as a combination of objectivity and perception, as a science and an art. Some studies demonstrate that how we appear to others is about more than what meets the eye. For example, one study examining the perception of beauty found that college students rated a professor as physically attractive when he behaved kind and friendly; whereas, when the same instructor behaved cold and distant, they did not.[7] In another study that examined attributes used to select a mate, physical features were viewed as having less value than qualities like seriousness, sincerity, and independence. For both men and women, finding a partner with whom they could develop a committed relationship was considered more important than finding one with good looks.[8] An international survey of women suggests that, in most countries, only a small percentage are comfortable calling themselves beautiful, but many call themselves attractive if they are engaged in enjoyable activities and have close relationships.[9]

In our own research, when we asked women the question, *"At what time in your life did you view yourself as most attractive?"* the answers were remarkably unrelated to age. A majority said it was in their 20s or 30s, but many responded that they felt most attractive later in life, when they felt more confident or when they were happiest.

•   •   •

**Findings from our studies and others on beauty confirm what most of us know: that experience of attractiveness is about what is outside and inside, and what counts most is connecting the two. And it is this very connection that millions of us are finding so hard to make.**

•   •   •

It might help to take comfort in the fact that our physical ideal of beauty holds greater contradictions today than ever before. Women sporting holes in jeans, rings through noses, and multicolored braids are seen on the covers of current fashion magazines. In contrast to traditional images which have been attributed to facial and body symmetry, there are now great varieties to what constitutes good looks: the ultra thin, ultra tall, the curvy, the bony, the straight haired, the curly, the spiky, and on it goes.

And public fascination with physical appearances currently flips as quickly as our remote controls—from Miss America to *The Biggest Loser*. When *America's Next Top Model* tried to broaden the criteria for their contestants by inviting women under 5' 7" to audition, they hoped to interest a greater variety of competitors seeking a spot on their show. The result? Bedlam broke out as hundreds of everyday, good-looking women flooded the audition, fighting for the chance to be acknowledged as the most beautiful.

You would think that all this opportunity and variety might represent a form of emancipation!

Yet among all these new variations there remains one constant that does not fluctuate in our culture or in our minds. *Youth.* Young, clear, unblemished skin and strong, smooth bodies remain the ideal image to which women feel driven. It is a visual ideal no longer confined to the province of young brides, celebrities, or fashion models. Women of all ages and walks of life are drawn toward this narrow definition of beauty at any cost and by whatever means.

• • •

**Instead of equality, we have this daunting equation: if beauty equals youth, and aging equals the loss of youth, then this is a new math that can't be mastered. Small wonder we are confused about the messages we are receiving and the emotions we did not think we would be confronting.**

• • •

Sure, millions turning 40 exhaled when feminist leader Gloria Steinem responded to being told that she didn't look her age with, *"This is what 40 looks like. We've been lying for so long, who would know?"* Yet ask most women and you will find that these milestones matter a great deal. With great fanfare, the toy industry celebrated Barbie's 50th birthday in 2009. Not surprisingly, this anatomically admired doll remains remarkably unchanged from the one we played with when we were little girls. Is this what we fought for? On paper we may claim it's unfair: why are we allowed to grow up but not grow older? Publicly we defy the inequity and deny the power of our youth-defined culture, while in reality it confronts us with enormous challenges and continues to be the road most sought by women of all ages.

## Coping with Changes That Keep On Changing

This challenge might be more manageable if not for the fact that women plan on living a whole lot longer than ever before. Until the beginning of the 20th century, life expectancy in the United States was 47 years.[10] Women were supposed to marry, bear children, and finish raising their families by the age we now call midlife. Up until the mid-1900s, a surprisingly large number of women never even made it past childbirth. Life after the children grew up wasn't even a consideration.

Fast-forward and we are the first generation likely to live well into our 80s and 90s. At age 40, some women are just beginning to think about starting families, having focused the first half of their lives on professional goals that were unavailable to women in previous generations. By the time we are grandmothers, we may either be too old to be changing diapers or too busy working—and working out—to want to be called granny. Clearly our experience of midlife has shifted our perspective about many issues, including our expectation to feel and look good as we age.

How we are coping with our evolving and extended lives reveals some distressing data. The number of plastic surgeries has not only increased dramatically, but perhaps even more disturbing is the average age of the women who now undergo these procedures. In 2008, more than 10.6 million surgical and nonsurgical procedures were performed on women, 2.2 million of them on women between the ages of 19 and 34. Women as young as 16 are now seeking cosmetic surgery to avoid the changes anticipated with aging.[11] With an expanding patient population, it's no surprise that dermatology today is considered the most sought-out specialty in medicine. Physicians—and often non-physicians—are supporting the growing trend among younger and younger women seeking to avoid wrinkles altogether by providing Botox injections to teens as routinely as acne treatments. We have to ask ourselves: what kind of babies have the boomers wrought?

Another trend that is worrisome among midlife women is the increase in eating disorders. More women in their 40s, 50s, and 60s are compulsively over-exercising, obsessed with trying to stay thin with the perfect abs and muscled thighs of much younger athletes.[12] The statistics surrounding how many midlife women are suffering from anorexia or bulimia, and the vulnerability for early onset osteoporosis, are distressing. Many of these older women are hesitant to get help, ashamed to have an illness normally associated with teenagers. Some talk about feeling depressed and alone, emotions that are expressed in perhaps the most upsetting statistic—the increase in suicide rates among midlife adults, with the most significant being women.

What is happening here? Are we so distressed by the conflicting messages about who we have become physically that we just do not know how to keep on going psychologically? Or worse, when faced with the decades that lie ahead, is it that we don't want to go on anymore? Though it is too soon to know what all these growing trends really mean, it is clear that many women of our generation are currently feeling unhappy and agitated and dreading the future. This is not a concern that can be easily dismissed or tossed aside as inconsequential or irrelevant. Obviously, there are great consequences and a compelling desire for change, not only in what we see in the mirror, but more importantly, how we feel about ourselves as we age.

## The Dilemma Is in the Details

Looking closely at studies on women, aging, and beauty reveals that the statistics are confusing and conflicting. For example, surveys show ambivalence about how we envision ourselves with our new horizons. One opinion poll done for AARP among 50-year-old women reported that inner beauty was chosen as the most important factor in feelings of well-being at midlife.[13] On the surface, aging women stand firm by this sentiment, as Lauren Bacall did when she said, *"Your whole life shows in your face and you should be proud of that."* Or when Angelina Jolie said, *"I'm enjoying getting older. I'm looking forward to life affecting me."* Researchers confirm this attitude among everyday women they study, who repeatedly identify kindness, intelligence, competence, and wisdom as attributes that contribute to their definition of attractiveness at midlife.[14]

Yet other studies on middle-aged women reveal a very different perspective. One done by the American Society of Aesthetic Plastic Surgeons showed that there has been a 114 percent increase in the number of cosmetic surgeries performed in the United States since 1997, with midlife women undergoing more than any other age group. This statistic rises to 457 percent if it includes non-surgical cosmetic procedures and an astonishing 754 percent if referring to nonsurgical procedures alone.[15] If we keep in mind these are paid for out-of-pocket, we can only imagine the number were they to be covered by insurance. When women were asked if they would contemplate cosmetic surgery if these procedures were deemed safe and offered for free, the numbers rose exponentially. Which set of statistics and attitudes reveals the real truth about women's experience as we age?

Obviously both do. Overall, studies on midlife women support the idea that both our internal and external selves are no doubt important. The problem is, few studies—and few women—show us how to reconcile the two. This, after all, was not our moms' predicament. The way most of our mothers thought about their appearance and the way they lived their lives at 40, 50, or 60 is not the way we are living ours. If they enjoyed healthy lives, they pondered issues like the appropriateness of wearing pants or showing cleavage. Their debates were over whether or not to dye their hair—does she or doesn't she? We face different options—has she or hasn't she? Helena Rubinstein, the original grande dame of the cosmetic industry, advised her generation, *"There are no ugly women, only lazy ones."* Yet few of our forebears thought of hitting the gym as our can-do generation does now, working out, tightening abs, trying to fit into our daughters' tiny black dresses.

While those daughters will hopefully have it easier as they head down their midlife path, studies reveal that teens today have a hard time envisioning this phase of life. When asked about their futures, they easily see their 20s filled with careers, travel, and relationships. Many can picture themselves in their 30s and even some in their 40s, viewing these years as time for further professional and personal growth. Almost none can articulate what they may be doing in their 50s and 60s. The narrative comes up empty. This generation of young girls may have expanded lifelines, but not expanded imaginations for what these years will bring. And perhaps we bear some responsibility. Could it be that their multitasking mothers, unglued by the midlife experience, are making this phase of life seem so bleak? Have we forgotten that we are the models for how these women will see themselves in their future? Surely we would have appreciated more appealing models for aging gracefully, and now it is our turn.

## Helen Mirren, Where Are You?

Let's face it: men have it easier. They can become doting dads at 70 and grow beards to cover their sagging skin. Clearly—and perhaps unfairly—the self-esteem of boys is tied more to what they do and how they perform than how they look. One study on self-esteem showed that individuals who look in mirrors more often than those who do not report a higher tendency for self-criticism.[16] Guess which category women fall into? Apparently, reflections are used less for self-praise than self-criticism. Not only do men grow up feeling less preoccupied and pressured to maintain their youthful appearance but they look better in gray. But enough about them!

Wouldn't it be easier if our society tolerated female maturation the way some other cultures do? Chinese women are not only admired but also desired for their increased wisdom; the French for their ongoing sex appeal; the Swedes for their natural beauty. Tibetan women say they feel that their beauty only increases with the passage of time, from the day they are born until the day they die. The Brits admire Helen Mirren, the French revere Catherine Deneuve and Jeanne Moreau. Oh sure, we applaud Diane Keaton and Susan Sarandon and the courage of their crow's feet, but even they feel the effects of our culture. Recently Sarandon spoke about being an aging actress, *"You're constantly reminded that you've been replaced in the kingdom . . . I'm discovering that I'm vainer than I thought."* In America, women are barraged with messages to defy, deny, and buy, persuasive words written on pharmaceutical products and spoken by airbrushed models.

We know. We were those models. When we were in our 20s we were cast in television ads, portraying midlife wives and moms promising youth formulas aimed for women in their 40s and 50s. Don't these manufacturers know that illusions of agelessness ultimately lead the average woman toward feeling even less beautiful as she reaches for the unreachable?

• • •

**The fear of aging and the fear of becoming unattractive are inextricably linked and embedded in the minds of most women. And belief in this equation is rapidly increasing, especially in American culture.**

• • •

Let's face it: every day, many of us participate in perpetuating this state of affairs, seeking solutions in a corporeal calculus that doesn't add up. We owe it to ourselves, and the generations of women that follow, to expand and create new meanings to the words *beauty* and *aging*.

Perhaps it's time for a healthy new dose of sisterhood.

## A New Movement: Somewhere Between Feminism and Narcissism

For years, the women's movement focused on freeing more than half our population from the traps of sexism and discrimination. As a result, women today continue to crash higher glass ceilings and break new barriers at every turn. We are a proud generation, witnessed by the thunderous applause Hillary Clinton received as she acknowledged the *"18 million cracks"* her votes represented in the 2008 primary. But do we really think she ever stopped caring how she looked while doing all that crashing and breaking? Do any of us? No doubt even accomplished women feel stressed keeping pace with confident, resourceful younger women sneaking up from behind. The sooner we realize that our changing looks plays a real yet complex role in how we feel about ourselves, the better we will be able to manage. It's time we use our knowledge, experience, and fortitude to change the way we deal with our changing looks.

The good news is that we have created a society where, as successful women, we are mostly admired for our years of hard work. Look at the well-earned kudos handed to Condoleezza Rice, Peggy Flemming, Barbra Streisand, and Diane Sawyer, to name a few. These are not simply "beauty queens," but queens on a much broader scale. The bad news is that women are often marginalized if their experience shows on their faces. Colleagues whisper, *"She needs some work."* In the movie business, it's, *"We need a young Glenn Close."*

How much have female stereotypes really changed if, during Hillary Clinton's run for president, Rush Limbaugh can rhetorically ask his large listening audience, *"Will Americans want to watch a woman get older before their eyes on a daily basis?"* Have we really been liberated if more attention is paid to the contents of Sarah Palin's wardrobe than the content of her speeches? We only have to look at the 2009 list of the World's Most Powerful Women, compiled by *Forbes*, to be reminded of the struggles we still face. To our credit, we see multiracial, black and white, but how often do we find gray?

We propose a new movement that meshes feminism with—dare we say?—a bit of necessary narcissism. This fresh perspective does not call for being wedded to either of these philosophies, but it will require finding a healthy balance between them. It entails a change in attitude, perspective, and focus. It means caring for ourselves by allowing looks to matter but not so much that we forget to take care of our long-term, lifetime needs. In the end, our movement will lead you to a new kind of freedom that takes into account both our internal and external selves, naturally blending the two.

•  •  •

**As a generation, we worked hard to change the culture in which we live. Now it's time to find a more dignified, thoughtful approach to our changing looks—to detoxify the cultural messages custom-fitted to women's anxieties and talk out loud about the subject, openly and honestly.**

•  •  •

We need not confine this dilemma to the comforting couches of psychotherapists—although we welcome that as one option—nor should we dump it in the deft hands of plastic surgeons. The challenge is not about how *not* to look our age, nor is it about seeking miracles to help us flee the facts. Make no mistake, we are not anti-surgery, anti-potions or peels, or anything else that allows us to feel better about ourselves. We are anti-thoughtless, pressured reactions to changing looks. We want women, who have broken through in so many arenas, to make decisions in this area with a similarly clear head and realistic expectations. Getting older was never a walk in the park, but it is particularly frightful to a generation of women who planned to stay "forever young." Once an appealing notion, these words have become a mandatory mantra. The challenge:

can we keep youthful optimism in our hearts and minds while letting our faces follow their natural course?

We are strong, smart, and vital women who have been given the gift of time. Let's not waste another moment trying to stop the inevitable. Our clocks tick on no matter what we do—or don't do—to our faces and bodies. Instead, let us size up where we are physically and emotionally. Let's recognize the cultural confusion that makes it hard to move forward. Let's go beneath the surface so we can look thoughtfully at our options for dealing more effectively with aging. If you are willing to enlist in this new movement and let us guide you on this unexpected journey, you will be able to find a better balance and take advantage of the process described in the following chapters.

# chapter two

. . .

## Women Caught Off Balance

*Here's the real question: What do we have to do to place
more value on age? We have to value ourselves not for
what we look like but for the women we are.*

— Maya Angelou

### Stuck in the Beauty Paradox

Between evolutionary, biological, and cultural forces, our
generation has been caught off balance. With so much conspir-
ing to confuse us, regaining our equilibrium is no easy task. So,
let's get specific and psychological: Who are we as individuals
and what is really going on inside of us? And what do we need
to know as we prepare to climb the six steps toward feeling and
looking great for the rest of our lives?

Leslie, a 50-year-old, well-respected executive
in a large PR firm, was having a full-blown panic
attack, the kind she hadn't experienced in many
years. During a surprise birthday party organized by
her boss, she found herself hiding in the bathroom,
soaked in sweat as she glanced at herself in the mirror, convinced something bad was about to happen.
*"I feel as if I am losing control,"* she said. *"What is
happening to me?"*

Sixty-one-year-old Jamie, married with two children, couldn't stop thinking about her tennis instructor. When she signed up for a series of expensive private lessons, she was not just looking to improve her second serve. *"It doesn't make sense. I have a crush! I'm not thinking straight, and I'm worried I might actually do something I know I shouldn't."*

Barbara had been feeling depressed. At 42, she was divorced, recovering from her second plastic surgery. She wanted to figure out why she felt so down, but meanwhile was completely focused on how to ensure she could have a child before it was too late. *"I feel so lonely these days, I just need something to look forward to,"* she said.

There was Cathy, who in her 40s couldn't understand her sudden lack of interest in getting close to her husband sexually. *"Since giving birth to my baby, I feel so self-conscious about my body and uncomfortable having sex with my husband,"* she said. *"I rarely take my clothes off in front of him, and when I do, I make sure the lights are off."*

Patricia, a 51-year-old woman, was not sure why she was in constant battle with her teenage daughter, the latest one over sharing clothes. *"It's bad enough she borrows mine without asking,"* she said, *"but what's worse is they look better on her!"*

And then there was Alana. She was suffering from insomnia. She was awakened several times each night by vivid dreams about being pushed out of her job. Her face looked tired and sad. *"My work is what I'm all about. It's who I am, and I dread that moment when I'll be passed over by some younger version of myself."* Alana is a 25-year-old model.

Different predicaments. Different symptoms. Different feelings.

Yet all these women are trapped in a web we know all too well: caught between the role their physical being once played in their lives, and the shift they need to make as their lives and looks are changing. All feel confused by how much their appearance did or didn't matter and by how much it should or shouldn't now. All are shaken by the arrival of change and find they instinctively and psychologically protect themselves against it.

As predictable as this turbulence is, these women are unprepared for its force and intensity. These are not unstable women, nor are their preoccupations unique. A wide variety of women—working professionals, stay-at-home moms, married, single, divorced—are struggling to emerge from similarly conflicting emotions, surprised by the loss of control in their otherwise balanced lives.

## The Necessary Shift

As psychotherapists who were once professional models, we know what it's like to place a premium on our appearance, be viewed from that perspective, and emotionally adjust as the role of beauty changes in our lives. Now specializing in helping women deal with these issues, we have become aware that we have put our finger on a crucial event experienced by all women in the aging process. Our psychotherapy work has confirmed for us that the emotional shift made early in the lives of models, dancers, and actors is actually an accelerated and magnified form of what we all feel, especially at midlife.

Interestingly, no matter how much value a woman places on her appearance, or how little, the fact that looks change creates some degree of ambivalence. Aging may be one of those foreseeable facts of life—every woman at some point will lose her youthful appearance—yet it throws most us into some level of crisis.

. . .

**Whether a woman feels her appearance played a major or minor role in her identity, changing looks impact us all. Physical changes evoke psychological ones that strike at the core of what makes women feel vital, alive, and attractive.**

. . .

Our reactions are manifested at different times in life and in a complex variety of ways, as we see in Leslie's panic, Jamie's crush, Barbara's obsession, Cathy's self-consciousness, Patricia's envy, and Alana's insomnia. Sometimes the feelings go underground and are barely recognizable until brought into a woman's awareness. Sometimes anxiety and helplessness are clearly expressed, and a panicky demand to stop the clock results. For all, the blow to self-esteem leaves women emotionally uncomfortable, seeking relief, avoidance, and control over this vulnerable state of affairs.

Leslie's panic started at her birthday party, when she looked in the bathroom mirror. Although the anxiety seemed to come out of nowhere and spread throughout her whole body, she came to realize that the glance at her 50-year-old face led to fears about aging, surprisingly so, since her appearance had never been a priority. For all her vaunted smarts, she was not aware until then how much her self-image had been a source of confidence and had assured her the ability to compete in the world.

Jamie's crush on her tennis instructor rose out of her desire to feel more attractive and appealing to the opposite sex. To grab the attention of a hot young coach was the sign she needed to prove to herself that she hadn't lost her looks. She talked about having once been in great shape and was angered by critical comments her husband made about her recent weight gain, even though she knew they were true. Being in better shape than others—especially other younger women—had become the all important index for her self-esteem. She was seeking affirmation but didn't know where to find it.

Barbara needed to recognize that wanting to get pregnant was her way of holding on to a body young enough to be able to have a baby, in the same way she wanted a face young enough to look as if she could. Being able to reproduce was her badge of femininity, and she was not prepared to accept this change. She had always taken her youth for granted and now that she couldn't, she was scared of the changes she saw outside and felt inside.

Cathy only began to understand her lack of sexual interest when she connected it to the intolerance she felt toward her postpartum body. As she became aware that self-criticism and punitive judgment interfered with her ability to enjoy sex, she was freer to work on becoming more intimate with her husband.

Patricia had difficulty acknowledging that jealousy was contributing to the recent tension she felt with her daughter. She had to shift the focus from the battles between them to the one she was waging within—between letting go and holding onto her own youthful looks. As Patricia's feelings of envy receded, she began to take better care of herself and her relationship with her daughter improved dramatically.

Alana's loss of sleep and dread of looking older were the result of a lack of perspective, understandable given the world she lived in. Her profession, and moreover, her sense of self were intimately connected to her looks, so that at age 25, she prematurely faced the kind of anxiety that many women confront at midlife.

These moments of awareness and recognition of change—which we call our uh-oh moments—are pervasive. They strike in unexpected ways: when we're bothered by our first wrinkles or gray hairs; when the opposite sex begins to look elsewhere and we find we care; when our sexual prowess—let alone interest—wanes in our relationships and we realize we can't take it for granted anymore. Although most of us know these changes are coming and even anticipate a sense of loss, women wind up doing surprising and inexplicable things to run from the intensity of the emotional turbulence we feel.

These emotional reactions are strongly influenced by the role our looks play in our identity. For all of us, the formation of self-image is both a psychological and physical experience and is determined by many factors. Self-image becomes rooted in our identity early in childhood, remains relatively stable during the years after adolescence, and then undergoes change again in midlife. When there is a shift in self-image—in the very basic way we see ourselves—we feel something fundamental change within us, whether we are aware of its origin or not.

. . .

**The more we rely on external measures alone to try to control or halt these changes, the more we interfere with an internal process that allows us to move on. Ironically, in trying to control the natural evolution of our appearance, we actually end up feeling more out of control. We become frightened instead of confident, confused rather than clear, and look desperate instead of dignified.**

. . .

We will show you the route to managing and then mastering the turmoil that so often comes at this phase of life. We will bring you through the same process Leslie, Jamie, Barbara, Cathy, Patricia, and Alana have followed. We will encourage you to look inside so you can make thoughtful decisions about changes on the outside.

## Aging Isn't Our Enemy—Fear Is

You can only do battle if you know your enemy. So it is with emotional battles.

. . .

**The enemy women face at midlife is not aging itself. It is the confusion and anxiety we feel about aging and how it will affect our emotional and physical selves.**

. . .

You are successful in battle when you confidently face your enemy with a game plan based on knowledge. The knowledge you gain as you read *Face It* will give you a step-by-step plan that maps out how to manage your feelings about your changing appearance. Knowledge is power, and we need both as we move forward through the changes that confront us at this stage of our lives. Rather than conforming to trajectories foist upon us by our genetics, our history, or our culture, we can feel freer to make conscious, informed choices and create our own personal path.

Remember, the way we perceive ourselves over time is a complex, personal, and organic process. Our six-step process requires continual, subtle internal shifts that lead to more noticeable external ones. As you make these changes, we hope you will emerge feeling as Jane did. At 44, she came for help, having suffered low self-esteem and neglecting herself for many years. After going through the following process and working hard on these issues, she mentioned that she planned to get her teeth whitened. *"To be honest, I have only just begun really smiling and feeling so much better about myself,"* she confessed. Jane experienced a positive internal shift, which found its way to the surface and back again, reinforcing both looking *and* feeling good.

Or, perhaps you will relate to Cathy, the woman who wanted to understand the changes she felt after having children, especially her lack of libido. The six steps not only helped her regain her interest in sex, but she had more enthusiasm for life in general. She said, *"After my attitude toward my body changed, I came out of hiding. I was able to be playful and intimate with my husband, even more than I had been before having children. I think liking myself helped me look better and I looked better because I was happier."*

Your issues may be different than the women described above, and the choices you make as you care for yourself may not be the same. But by following our six steps, you can learn to feel similarly optimistic and comfortable. We don't condone impetuously whitening teeth, shopping for a new wardrobe, or purchasing any quick-fix remedy with money you don't have. We support both internal and external measures that make sense because they help you look as good as you feel.

. . .

**Ultimately we need to stop trying to halt time as we face the changes we see. Our goal is to move forward with time, internalizing a different lens through which to view ourselves, one that is kinder and more receptive to the changes we experience as we age.**

. . .

And that is exactly what our journey together is about.

# SECTION II

Six Steps to Change

# chapter three

• • •

## Uh-Oh Moments

*Perhaps one has to be very old before one learns to be amused rather than shocked.*

— Pearl S. Buck

## Step One: Moving Toward the Inside

It may be the first gray hair, or perhaps an offhand remark that feels surprisingly insulting, like, *"Do you have grandchildren?"* Welcome to your uh-oh moment, when you become cognizant for the first time that something fundamental about who you are as a woman is changing and will never be the same. Watching others age seems more gradual, while our own shift is jarring. As smart and evolved as we are, few of us are prepared for the moment when it arrives or the feelings it provokes. Few are willing to admit that it even matters.

The uh-oh moment is not a reason for running to the latest Ms. Fix-it remedy; rather, it signals that inner work is necessary to both diversify and solidify aspects of our sense of self. Many women we're seeing at midlife are feeling depressed or anxious after years of living seemingly satisfying lives. Sometimes family members suggest they talk to a therapist, since they're not acting like themselves. Most can't figure out why, but they know they just don't feel right.

When we see these women in our practices, we first ask why they've come for help and begin with what is on their minds. We know that uh-oh moments can be confused with other thoughts and feelings that may not emerge right away. So we ask our patients to tell us their stories and encourage them to be as open and honest as possible. We establish a relationship and atmosphere that allows women to feel comfortable. We carefully observe them and listen closely to what they have to say. We're interested in hearing what lies on the surface first— like thoughts about the important people in their lives, what interests them, the lifestyles they lead and the work they do. As we move inward, we listen carefully to their feelings and concerns and ask not only about their present, but their past as well. We listen to the attitude, tone, and meaning behind their words. We also listen to what is not being said.

Beth, for example, considered herself the kind of woman whose appearance stayed in the background of her active and successful life, until she couldn't ignore her reaction to her changing face.

A 52-year-old educator, she had dropped by a photo shoot her husband was directing. *"I had always prided myself on being above the superficiality of the fashion world, so I was confused by the tailspin of emotions I felt afterwards. I felt uneasy for a couple of weeks following that visit, but I couldn't put my finger on why."* Beth found herself focusing on the lines around her eyes and mouth, though she hadn't paid an undue amount of attention to them before. She told us she went home that day, found herself facing her bathroom mirror, making sure no one was looking and pulled back her skin to see what she'd look like were she to get work done.

Beth was not only taken by surprise by her uh-oh moment, she was confused by the feelings that followed. *"I don't know why my visit that day had such an impact. I've watched my husband work before, often with beautiful women, but as I saw him enjoy photographing the models, it just made me uneasy. I think that's what got me looking in the mirror."*

Whether you've anticipated the experience or it takes you by surprise, as it did Beth, the uh-oh moment can be experienced in a variety of ways, from vague discomfort and anxiety to panic and depression. While one woman may feel a mild ominous uneasiness resembling tremors before a quake, another's reaction may be more akin to the quake itself. As one woman said on her way to her third round of plastic surgery, *"I'm not afraid of dying so much as I'm afraid of living looking old."* No doubt for this woman and others like her, the aftershocks of fear, both physical and psychological, continue long after their first tremulous uh-oh moment.

Before we can take the first step toward changing the way we feel about our changing looks, we need to understand a basic psychological principle: with awareness and acknowledgment of our true feelings, change is more likely to occur. Avoidance makes emotional growth very difficult and highly unlikely.

• • •

**If we do not understand the source and meaning of our negative feelings about looking and feeling older, we may find ourselves emotionally stuck and behaving irrationally. We react without thinking and take action without using good judgment.**

• • •

Instead of attempting the impossible—trying to stop time—we need to learn how to use our increased awareness of our uh-oh moment and our understanding of the reactions that follow. It is the path toward gaining a greater sense of calm and control over what is to come. Most of us ignore these initial feelings or convince ourselves there must be something more substantial at play. We tend to feel ashamed that we have such feelings at all or humiliated that they matter so much. As a result, we all too frequently keep them from others or mistakenly muddle them with generalized irritability, anxiety, and depression. In fact, most women who have passed through this difficult phase tell us that these moments are unforgettable, as much as we'd like to forget them.

## Reading Your Feelings Between the Lines (No, Not Those Lines!)

Once you acknowledge uh-oh moments without judgment, you will become acutely aware of them in yourself and others. If you recognize them as turning points, rather than warnings to run for your life, you will be able to use them productively. We have, in the stories of hundreds of women like you, like us.

As you might expect, few clients come to therapy to get help for their uh-oh moments. There is no category in the Diagnostic and Statistic Manual used by psychotherapists for "psychological problems as a result of changing looks," while there are categories for almost every other major transition in life: adjustments related to marital issues, work, finances, and losses of all kinds. This is unfortunate because there is clear, statistical proof that women suffer unhappiness and low self-worth as a result of feeling unattractive; and few women seek help directly for this issue.[17]

Although the media inundates us with new cures and solutions for aging skin, hair, and teeth, a deeper exploration of beauty rarely finds its way into intellectual conversation or directly into therapeutic discussion. As we listen to women's stories, the struggles are there between the lines.

Take Denise for example:

Denise was thinking about leaving her husband of 30 years. She said, *"I still love him, but almost everything he does bothers me."* She was irritable around him, found herself snapping at him and didn't really know why. *"He ignores what I say, I get critical of him, and then he ignores me even more. I don't see a way out."* She told us that until recently they had many years of relative compatibility, negotiating typical marital conflicts as they both worked hard and raised three children together. *"Something this past year has changed,"* Denise said.

We asked the usual therapists' questions: What was going on that may have led to these changed feelings? What might be going on at her work? How did Denise feel about the children leaving home? What about her sex life? At some point we asked Denise a question therapists don't often ask: how do you feel about how you look these days? Denise responded with surprise and slight annoyance. *"What does that have to do with anything?"* As therapists often do, we responded to her question with one of our own. *"Does the way you look matter to you?"*

As if given permission to talk about some feelings she had kept secret from herself, Denise's emotions came pouring out. She said she knew that entering her 50s had been difficult for her and her irritability and critical attitude toward her husband seemed connected to that turning point. We asked if there was a moment or an experience she could identify that provoked these feelings. It was like an "ah-ha" moment, but clearly an uh-oh one, when Denise recalled how she felt one morning, after putting on her makeup. *"I went out the door, saw myself in the elevator mirror and did a double take. For a moment I thought I had forgotten to put on my makeup. Then I realized I did have makeup on. I was just old and cosmetics couldn't cover my aging face. I realized then nothing would.*

When Denise allowed her feelings about her changing looks to matter, it opened up a well of emotions she hadn't shared with anyone. She told us she couldn't tell her husband, because *"he wouldn't understand."* Although she talked to her friends about aging in general, she was embarrassed by the intensity of her feelings. She knew she had become overly sensitive about the whole topic of looking older, but she didn't realize that these feelings were contributing to her recent irritability and unhappiness, and that they were spilling over into her marriage. She was upset, believing her husband was no longer attracted to her, but in fact, her distress was in part rooted in no longer feeling attractive.

It wasn't just that her appearance was changing. It was the feelings these changes generated and how they were affecting her relationships. Not since her youth had Denise's sense of security been so overshadowed by self-doubt. Not since then had her emotional ground felt so shaky.

## Now You See You, Now You Don't

Clearly, simply being aware of uh-oh moments and the feelings they evoke isn't the solution to either marital issues, like Denise's, or the discomfort felt by millions of women as they confront their changing looks. It's a beginning. Most women coming for psychotherapy often seek help with some life struggle: a relationship that isn't working, family problems, a career that is no longer satisfying. Sometimes symptoms like insomnia, panic or an eating disorder are presented, but uh-oh moments get us started on a topic that is not easily discussed, even in therapy.

• • •

**Step one, acknowledging your uh-oh moment means accepting that an ostensibly surface reaction to your changing looks is connected to a much more complicated set of feelings—feelings about one's life, its limitations, and the future.**

• • •

At some point, as we did with Denise and Beth, we bring women's attention to how they feel about the way they look. Some react with surprise. Some are even offended by a question of seemingly trivial importance. We remind them that to a certain degree, their self-image—how they see themselves and how they feel others see them—is integral to their identity and sense of worth. We tell them that the picture they have of themselves is not based simply on objective details like height, weight, and hair color, but on what they have internalized about themselves from personal experience. We assure them that how they look *physically* is less important to us than how they *feel* about their looks, and that their feelings about their appearance are very important. They ask, *"You mean I can talk about that here?!"*

We tell them that in therapy, as in real life, many women feel paradoxical pulls about beauty and that any discussion regarding looks will be challenged by these culturally conflicting forces. We encourage them to say whatever is on their minds, without censorship, so that together, we can look back, look inward, and look forward to making an about face. We tell them that this is especially important as they confront their uh-oh moment. A topic that up until now was felt to be unworthy of discussion, becomes one of clear importance in the understanding of ourselves as we age.

 .  .  .

**As we allow more value and meaning to be placed on uh-oh moments, the door opens for beauty to be part of a deeper discussion about our emotional selves. It brings awareness that these moments are really confrontations with basic existential issues—feelings about potential loss and the loss of potential—and, though set off by changes on our faces and bodies, the feelings spread throughout our entire beings.**

 .  .  .

## The Cutting Truth of Words

We now can move inward. We listen closely as women begin talking more openly about their uh-oh moments, set off not only by glances in mirrors, but occasionally by something said to them.

Delia's 75-year-old mother often made critical comments which Delia had learned to let roll off her back. One memorable insult, after Delia sadly announced that her husband was leaving her, was hard to ignore. Her mother said, *"Well, what do you expect? You look older than his mother!"* Delia believed this was probably true, so her mother's words stung. Sadness that started over her failed marriage became mixed with an uh-oh moment that she couldn't shake. She felt scared about what her future held, as a middle-aged new divorcée.

Wendy had her uh-oh moment when her 5-year-old son innocently asked, *"What are those stripes on your forehead, Mommy?"* Although she laughed at his adorable comment about her less-than-adorable face, she also felt a sense of anxiety as she confronted being an older parent. Instead of the gratitude she usually felt at becoming a mom so late in life, she focused on her worry and anticipation of looking like her son's grandma as he grew up.

Marion had a solid relationship with her husband. But she felt her heart sink when he innocently asked, *"What are those spots on your hand, honey?"* helping her clasp a bracelet he bought for their anniversary. *"I felt ashamed, almost as if the secret I had successfully hidden from my own husband of 30 years was out. I was old."*

People who are important to us can unwittingly reinforce cultures' paradoxical messages about beauty and aging. Delia's mother added anxiety to her daughter's feelings about her marriage difficulties, focusing the cause of its failure on her aging looks. Like so many who automatically "trust" the wisdom of elders, Delia bypassed the gratuitous cruelty of the remark and responded as if it were credible. Even though Wendy's son likely saw his mommy as the most beautiful woman in the world, and would be upset if she did anything to alter her looks, his comment reinforced her concerns about being perceived as an older mother. Marion's husband seemed oblivious that his comment would instill insecurity in his wife, but clearly it did.

Comments about women's faces and bodies can have long-lasting repercussions and sometimes come from unexpected and unacceptable sources. One woman recalls a friend of her parents, a plastic surgeon, telling her as a teenager that he would be happy to "do her nose." When she saw him at a recent holiday dinner his words still rankled her three decades later. "I still am completely self-conscious about my nose," she admits at 56, "but this time I asked him what he thought about doing my whole face!"

Felice's uh-oh moment was stirred by a physician, an authority figure who should surely know better.

Felice, a 30-year-old lawyer, went for a routine visit to her gynecologist. She began talking about possibly having her tubes tied, since she didn't want any more children. When the doctor said *"perhaps you might consider having your breasts lifted too since you won't be nursing again,"* she wasn't sure how to respond. She hadn't thought her breasts were unattractive, but if this 55-year-old doctor did, she wondered if her husband did too. She went home that day and took a more careful look. *"I guess I didn't realize how droopy they were. But my whole body is drooping, so where would I start?"*

As Felice described the exchange she had in the doctor's office, she realized she was more irritated than anxious by the "breast lift" comment. She was well aware that she was facing issues about her changing body and getting older. It was why she wanted a tubal ligation. She had been thinking that no more children meant she could work out more, have more time to herself, and get her body into the best shape possible. Fortunately, by understanding the uh-oh feelings the doctor provoked with his insensitive remark, Felice was able to recognize this was *his* issue, not hers.

Whether they come innocently from the mouths of babes, loving husbands, or professionals who care for us, uh-oh moments are hard to ignore when provoked by another. Sometimes, it's not in the words people say, but the way others treat—or ignore—us that cause our uh-oh moments to rise to the surface. We may still see ourselves as youthful and flirtatious—and justifiably *feel* that way—but when *others* respond to our changing looks in a way that is dissonant with our own experience of ourselves, it can throw us off balance.

Carol, a single woman aged 43 was sipping wine at her law firm's holiday party. She was joined by one of her partners, Tom, who was about her age. They were having fun, enjoying a break from endless late nights working on a difficult case they shared. When Carol realized Tom's wife wasn't there, she asked why. He said that they had *"just separated and were going through an ugly divorce."* Carol said she was sorry, and then wondered if it explained the recent flirtation she felt between them. When she asked if he was doing all right, he said, *"Oh, don't worry about me. I'm looking forward to meeting one of these cute chicks that intern here."* She hoped her face didn't show the arrival of her uh-oh moment. Shaken, she thought to herself, *"I'm too old to even be on his radar screen! What was I thinking?"*

Confrontation with uh-oh moments can burst our bubble. Carol's moment came when she realized that because of her age, the fantasy she had was hers alone. When the image we have of ourselves conflicts with the way others see us, it not only catches us off guard, but it can feel crushing. It forces into awareness the fundamental shift in our identities we are frequently unprepared to accept.

**EXPERIENCES THAT SPARK UH-OH MOMENTS**

• • •

First wrinkles—crow's feet, smile lines

Drooping eyelids

Darkening circles below eyes

Graying and thinning hair

Receding hairline

Yellowing teeth

Needing to shave or wax less frequently

First white lash or eyebrow hair

Darkening moustache line above the top lip

Brown spots on hands and face

Loss of muscle tone, changing body shape, cellulite

Varicose veins

Hanging skin on arms, neck

Hot flashes

Last menstrual cycle

Decreasing interest in or increasing discomfort during sex

## Uh-Oh Stories: One Size Does Not Fit All

Uh-oh moments can strike at any time, unrelated to our chronological age. Some women, like Deborah, experience this relatively early in life.

Deborah was 36 when she noticed her hair seemed as if it was getting lighter during the summer months.

Being a blonde, she liked the highlights she believed were coming out under the sun. But as they remained all winter, she wasn't sure she liked what she saw. At first she began to pull out the gray hairs, one by one, and by age 38 she found herself pulling out too many to avoid the reality. It was time to color her hair. When her hairdresser eagerly started showing Deborah the color chart, it hit her like a jolt. *"She sees it too. I am going gray. I'm not even middle-aged. But if I don't do something, I will look old even if I don't feel old."*

Some of us have good genes, some of us have genes that aren't as good—but aging happens to everyone, so there is little point in keeping score. We have remarkably different biological timetables and our reactions to them have even greater variability. For most women, however, the uh-oh moments occur in midlife.

Helen was an active woman at age 62, working as an executive in an insurance company. She felt her looks were important to her. They made her feel good about herself and she made sure to stay in shape. She often thought that the only good thing about being single and childless was that she still had her youthful-looking body, no sagging breasts or loose stomach. One day at the gym she noticed her arms looked different as she lifted weights. She looked closely. *"It almost felt like my arms, and the skin hanging from them, didn't belong to me."* She worked her upper body regularly and hadn't noticed anything until that day. Her uh-oh moment came as she realized, no matter how much she worked out, her arms no longer responded to exercise the way they once had. They were changing, as was the rest of her body. *"I am embarrassed and ashamed to admit how depressed I felt."*

Deborah, 36, and Helen, 62, were both confronting the kinds of losses that emerge into consciousness with uh-oh moments. Deborah, whose hair was losing its color and Helen, whose body was losing its muscle tone, had their moments when their bodies forced them to face life's limitations. Both were part of a generation that was once offended at the whistles on the street. Now they wouldn't mind just a few!

At 56, Cory liked to take walks with her 15-year-old daughter. *"Sometimes people say we look and act a lot alike. I love it when on occasion I hear that we look like sisters."* Although Cory was in her late 50s, she could keep pace with her daughter. One summer morning, as they walked the city streets in shorts and tank tops, Cory returned with a pit in her stomach. *"I realized for the first time that people's stares were focused on my daughter's body, not mine."* She felt her uh-oh moment as the mother of, not the object of, people's stares.

## Turning Uh-oh into Ah-ha

The more overwhelmed we feel by our uh-oh moments, the more we end up generating the very experience we're trying to avoid. By attempting to flee these distressing emotions, we actually create more tension and the less it becomes us. Uh-oh can only become ah-ha if we acknowledge what we feel and face it, gain confidence in our reasonable reactions, and turn passive fear into productive action.

Remember Felice? The woman whose visit to her gynecologist provoked her uh-oh moment? His suggestion that she surgically change her breasts was disquieting, but instead of reacting impulsively, she used her uh-oh moment for insight. Although she recognized her doctor had uncomfortably reminded her of her aging body, she didn't dwell on the discomfort, or rush to schedule a plastic surgery consultation. She felt this concern was more her doctor's than hers. She acknowledged that her breasts were no longer perky, and like other parts of her body, didn't look as they once had. But she was also proud of her experiences as a mother and felt her body reflected her hard work nurturing her children.

This awareness allowed Felice to begin to transform uh-oh to ah-ha. Instead of plastic surgery as a way to deal with her changing looks, Felice became determined to get into better shape and pay more attention to herself. She accepted that her body would change—and that people like her doctor might notice—but she was not willing to accept losing her sense of attractiveness. She wanted to move on to the next step and was on her way.

Some women, like Felice, can turn their uh-oh feelings around quickly. For others it takes more time. But the emotions are shared by many and there is a reason why. Although our appearance may be skin deep, our self-image is not. Every person's appearance—male, female, young, and old—is integral to identity. Outside of the biological features that distinguish us from men, our set of physical features are unique only to us and strongly influence the way we think, store information, and absorb the world around us. From that perspective, how we look is not a superficial aspect of ourselves at all and will be discussed further in Step Four when we describe how self-image develops. The uh-oh moment is an important step—the first—along our way. We have a chance to turn uh-oh into ah-ha if the sting of awareness can be absorbed, understood, and integrated, rather than denied or dismissed.

To be sure, this sting of awareness strikes celebrities and everyday women alike; the former often suffer too publicly, the latter too privately. On national television, Elizabeth Edwards spoke candidly about her emotional turmoil after learning that her husband, John, 2008 presidential candidate, had an affair. In addition to her feelings of hurt and anger, she confessed that his infidelity led to a sudden self-consciousness and insecurity about her age, weight, and appearance. While the pain over her husband's betrayal was expected, the uh-oh moment accompanying it took her by surprise.

TV journalist Connie Chung knows all too well about public scrutiny of the aging process. Constantly judged by a fickle world of viewers and critics, she told us about her uh-oh moment: *"I first started seeing age in the mirror when I got what I call the 'bowser' look; jowls that wiggle when I shake my head, jowls like a slobbering old dog who looks at you with droopy eyes and utters rr-wuff, rr-wuff."*

Whether we perform on the screen or live in the mainstream, all women's bodies and faces change as we age. Although it is a universal experience, change is particularly difficult for women in Western society. We celebrate many transitions in life, like graduations, confirmations, bat mitzvahs, weddings, pregnancies. Yet we watch people pass through the latter part of their lives with little or no celebration of that achievement. Merry Menopause, anyone?

Life is about moving through stages and not getting stuck in one, which is not to be confused with getting the most out of every current stage. Actors Jessica Lange and Meryl Streep set good examples. In a commencement speech at Sarah Lawrence College, Lange suggested, *"Be present and open to the moment that is unfolding before you. Because, ultimately, your life is made up of moments. So don't miss them by being lost in the past or anticipating the future. Don't be absent from your own life."* She is someone who, having left her ingenue stage behind and facing uh-oh moments along the way, has managed to navigate aging with grace and finesse.

When Streep won the Golden Globe for *The Devil Wears Prada* in 2006, she inadvertently displayed her aging process as she took the stage. After fanning herself from what seemed like a hot flash, she took a deep breath and spoke eloquently about her gratitude for receiving great roles *even* at her age. In what appeared to be a potentially uncomfortable uh-oh moment in front of millions, she gracefully, humorously, and poignantly embraced her age and beauty all at once. Streep, as always, wore pure class.

For all women, well known or not, every physical experience of aging has a psychological component. Which particular physical change is most momentous and disturbing differs for each of us—wrinkles, crow's feet, skin spots, hot flashes—the list is long. Although there are many variations to the uh-oh theme, each can ignite deep reactions that arrest you in your tracks and have ramifications that need to be understood before you can move forward. Recognizing your own uh-oh moment, and knowing what it means to you, is a first step. It is in the identification of your fear, the recognition of the unknown and the awareness of impending loss that helps you gain understanding and a sense of control over this next phase of your life.

## Using Your Uh-oh Moment to Move Toward the Inside

- When was the first time you noticed your looks were changing?

- What did you think? How did you feel? How did you react?

- Do you look in the mirror constantly? Do you avoid looking?

- Do you discard photographs of yourself these days?

- What is your reaction when you see others looking at you?

- When you identify your uh-oh moment, try to use it to recognize that you, like many women, are experiencing a transition into a new phrase of your life.

- Acknowledge that your looks are changing. It will lead you to learn how to manage this transition with less fear and more confidence.

# chapter four

· · ·

## Masks

*The closing years of life are like the end of a masquerade party, when the masks are dropped.*

— Arthur Schopenhauer

## Step Two: Getting Underneath

We are smart women with serious concerns. No doubt, a sagging economy poses a more ominous threat than sagging skin. And arthritic feet take precedence over crow's feet. But, let's face it: these concerns are not mutually exclusive. In fact, more "acceptable" issues can sometimes distract us from the true source of our angst. To move toward redefining a sense of beauty for the next chapter of your life, it's important to become aware of the possible ways you may be distancing yourself from uncomfortable feelings about your changing looks.

These out-of-character behaviors and emotional reactions are protective measures we call "masks," functioning to psychologically deny and physically defy aging. Though masks can provide a means to temporarily hold onto an outdated sense of self by mummifying a natural process, they also keep us stuck and unable to acknowledge our true emotions. Enter Step Two: identifying and removing our masks.

Julie noticed her menstrual cycle changing—an uh-oh moment for many women. She had looked forward to a life without the hassles of tampons and mood swings, but instead she found herself down in the dumps and harboring surprising new feelings. *"All I can think about lately is having another child,"* she said. When she was asked if her husband had the same desires, Julie confessed, *"He thinks I am crazy and says he's done with child rearing. He's says he's worried about the stress another child would put on our finances and my health. But I'm only 45. I have two kids and I could handle one more."*

The more Julie's preoccupation with child rearing was explored, the more she began to talk about deep feelings of sadness. She felt she had the solution. *"I want to see fertility doctors. My husband won't go with me, but I have been off the pill and nothing is happening. I can't stop looking at mothers with their baby strollers and it makes me cry."* We asked Julie to tell us how she felt about other parts of her life, including her appearance. *"I'm stressed and I know my face shows it. I just cannot tolerate the thought of never having another baby,"* she said. It seemed that being able to bear children made Julie feel powerful and the dread of the male equivalent of impotence was the drive behind wanting another child. *"When I was pregnant, I felt I was at my best. I felt so full of life and productive."*

It became obvious that being pregnant also had made Julie feel beautiful. She showed us pictures of herself during her three pregnancies, saying that she looked most attractive to herself during those times. She did not want to face the idea that her youth was fading and found the time-consuming quest to have another child soothing in a certain way, even if she'd be risking her marriage and health in the process. Here is the problem: when you cling to a peak time, you find yourself holding onto an experience of yourself from the past. Our work was to help Julie understand how the focus on fertility served to help her avoid strong feelings about aging and about looking and feeling older that lay right beneath the surface.

As Julie talked she began to see the connection between the urgency to have another baby and her emotional reaction to her fading youth.

> She said, *"Although I honestly wanted to have another child, I had no idea it was coming from so many other feelings. It was so powerful, I couldn't think straight. When I started to think of ways to have a baby without my husband's consent, I knew I was acting crazy. I guess I was hoping to use a rocking chair for a baby rather than for myself."*

Finally, when she felt ready, Julie shared her dilemma with her husband. She explained that she had always seen life in two polarities: young (can have baby) and old (can't have baby). Understanding this gave the couple a starting point for better communication, equipped now to define this phase of life in new terms.

## Why We Wear Masks

When women recognize that no personal action halts the process of aging, they feel vulnerable and powerless. To manage these feelings, women often use masks. Much the way people universally deal with the fears of change or of the unknown, women use masks reflexively, as measures of protection. And often it takes effort to uncover what they're hiding. Especially when they are displaced onto others.

> Cynthia, a 51-year-old single mother, works as an aide in an assisted living facility. She loves her job, saying, *"I've always felt like I do God's work, helping the elderly as if they were my own parents."* She came for help because she was concerned about being overly protective of the ladies she was caring for. She had been waking up with dreams that they had died over-

night. She described dressing and adorning her clients with makeup and jewelry with great care, doing and redoing their hair. She said *"My concerns are getting in the way of being caring and loving the way I used to be. I even got irritated the other day when one of the ladies I adore spilled coffee on her shirt. I keep thinking that they're going to die. I know it seems strange, since I've been at this job for 15 years."*

We explored the reasons why Cynthia's feelings about work had changed and what she expressed were feelings about her own aging. She hadn't spent much time caring for herself, her looks, or her health; and when she turned 50, she started to notice that everyone she saw outside of work seemed younger than she felt. And at work, she could only see her own future and it didn't appear rosy. *"My son left for college and I kept thinking he'd be visiting me in a facility like this not too long in the future."* Cynthia found focusing on her clients' aging and future more palatable than paying attention to her own, but it was her own that required her attention.

Cynthia had years of living ahead of her, but saw this midpoint not as the beginning of the next phase, but as a finale. Reaching 50, Cynthia felt like many women approaching milestone birthdays—40, 50, or 60. They don't see it as aging a year; they feel as if they've aged a decade, careening toward the end of their lives. For Cynthia, the very notion that she would be "in her 50s" was devastating. The problem for both Cynthia and Julie was that their perception of what constitutes "old" had not caught up with the possibilities available to midlife women today.

If in our practices we see a pattern, it is this: many women exhibit behaviors, emotions, and symptoms that reflect and camouflage feelings about how their looks are changing.

• • •

Step Two is learning to identify the masks we use not only to cushion ourselves against the discomfort of aging, but to keep us from acknowledging that we care. By diverting, distracting, displacing, and projecting, the masks we use to cover our feelings can make the underlying anxiety, shame, and dread easier to tolerate temporarily.

• • •

Yet masks are ultimately ineffective in protecting against the intangible dread and inevitable reality of aging. And, unfortunately, they also keep us from gaining access to what is truly going on. Let's look more carefully at what lies behind these masks and why we wear them.

## Masks That Are Hard to See

The masks we're describing aren't the same as those we don for Halloween. Nor are they the kind of "new" faces that women like Joan Rivers candidly try on every year or so. The key difference is that these masks are not voluntary and at times they are not even in our conscious awareness. They arise out of an emotional need, not a physical one.

Mindy had been feeling out-of-sorts for a while. Now at 61, she said she became aware of her uh-oh moment when she realized it had been weeks since a co-worker had come by to flirt. She reacted as she had at other times in her life, by taking action. She went on a shopping spree. *"I found myself thinking I needed to spice up my look. I became obsessed with looking through magazines, thinking of the new outfits I should buy that might make me look just a bit younger and sexier."* She started by spending extra money she couldn't really afford. After that, she decided a cheaper tactic was to use outfits tucked in the back of her closet from years

## FOUND IN TRANSLATION

• • •

Here are a few examples of ways women mask feelings about their changing looks.

**Mask:** "My husband no longer finds me sexy since I turned 60."
**Translation:** You may think you no longer look sexy or appealing, so you project these thoughts onto your husband and assume he feels that way. If so, no matter what your husband says or does, you take it as confirmation of that belief.

**Mask:** "I'm obsessed with the idea of having a fourth child and can't let it go. I'm determined to get pregnant, even though I'm 45 and my husband would have to reverse his vasectomy."
**Translation:** Although you may truly want another child, perhaps it's worth looking at the possibility that this desire masks feelings about aging.

**Mask:** "I have so much work to do at the office; I don't have time to work out or care how I look."
**Translation:** It's easier to focus on work than deal with the changes you see on your face and body. You may be using your work as an excuse not to take care of yourself.

**Mask:** I'm wearing my daughter's clothes because mine are all in the laundry."
**Translation:** You may be feeling and looking older and want to appear younger, but don't want to accept these feelings, so you find ways to rationalize them.

**Mask:** "I think women should take a practical approach to aging. After all, everyone gets older; it's just a fact of life."
**Translation:** You may be turning feelings into facts and trying to keep it all cerebral. We all know that women have feelings about getting older, but you won't let yourself connect to your emotions.

**Mask:** "I used to care about my looks, but now I'm married and in menopause. Besides, I like junk food and it's liberating not to care."
**Translation:** You may have convinced yourself that looks don't matter anymore, because you're settled in your life. But you may have gained weight and are scared that you've lost control, not only over your eating habits but over your body as well. If you no longer feel you can rely on beauty as a source of self-esteem, you may be masking this experience with not caring at all.

**Mask:** "I do my shopping by mail order. I can't deal with stores and salespeople. I'm not that into fashion anyway."
**Translation:** Shopping online is convenient, especially if you want to avoid dressing room mirrors and your changing looks.

ago, even though they didn't fit her anymore. Mindy said, *"I even started borrowing my daughter's clothes . . . my quest for the right outfits to get the right reactions became an obsession and I just couldn't think about anything else."*

We suggested that Mindy think about what feelings might have provoked her shopping spree. As we talked to Mindy further, it became clear that her obsession with the "right" clothes was less about the outfits and more about managing her anxiety. Shopping was Mindy's attempt to gain control over her feelings about being unable to attract her co-worker's attention. But all that accessorizing was distracting her from facing her feelings about aging. We helped her see that transitioning from a flirtatious young adult to a mature but still attractive woman, was a rite of passage, not a kiss of death.

Mindy's shopping habit had been with her for a long time and like many measures we use to protect ourselves from our feelings, they often evolve in childhood when our minds and emotional lives are developing. They impact how we interpret and perceive the world. Even as we age and our thinking matures, our coping mechanisms—or masks—often don't change and remain linked to earlier stages in life. It's one of the reasons why smart people can say and do things that seem childish and foolish.

Clothes held many meanings for Mindy. They reminded her of childhood bonding experiences with her mother. And being dressed up attracted attention and made her feel that she stood out. She experienced these same feelings when her co-worker flirted with her, and without them, she felt invisible—much as we could surmise she had felt in her childhood. For Mindy, aging was associated with being undesirable, less visible, and, underneath it all, less important. And that feeling is what she ultimately wanted to control.

. . .

**Clinging to an illusion of physical youth often leads to reliance on the approval of others to validate that illusion. Women's sense of beauty is then too dependent on external sources, rather than an internal experience. We can do better than that if we look behind our masks.**

. . .

As women recognize that trying to return to someone we once were leads to measures that can only fail, we can feel sad but relieved as well. Mindy said, *"I know on some level I couldn't go back to the way I once was, but I was afraid to look forward."* Facing the feelings behind masks is less overwhelming once we know what we are running from.

## Are You Wearing a Mask?

Some masks are more apparent than others, like Mindy's attempts to look young through the clothes she wore. Some are harder to recognize, like Cynthia's increased focus on caring for her clients. Some masks are impulsive and instinctive, like covering your eyes when you see a horrific scene. They can materialize so quickly and automatically that we don't even know they're on. Masks most difficult to identify are those that come disguised or muddled with other emotions, like generalized irritability, the "blahs," or hypersensitivity.

Let's look at Fran.

Fran is a hard-working vice president of an online magazine. Everyone in her office worked in one large loft-like room. *"I always loved that aspect of my job, being all together, working together, but recently I'm feeling paranoid and irritated by everyone. Maybe I just don't like people!"* Being 42, she was at the older end of the age group working on the magazine. She had been one of the founding members. *"I have to admit I was a workaholic when the magazine got off the ground. It was like my baby, which is why I don't understand why people don't want me around. The other day, everyone went off to have drinks and they didn't ask me to join them. I was pissed. But, who cares, they're babies and stupid. I'm not sure I care about anything much these days. I'm no fun anymore."*

Fran had recently become more sensitive to the fact that the dot-com world had become younger and younger. What she couldn't see was that her co-workers adored her, loved her sense of humor and her ability to give advice, and rarely thought about their age difference. Her irritability and sensitivity were a reaction to the work environment, as she perceived it. She realized that when she felt ignored and rejected, she would mask her hurt feelings by responding with hostility and rejection—a method of coping she had adopted in her childhood.

Do Fran's masked emotions and reckless actions ring a bell? Have you been hypercritical of your peers, husband, or children? Are you especially sensitive to criticism from others? Have you considered having an affair with a younger man—or any man, for that matter? Are you preoccupied with making social, renovation, or travel plans to keep from staying in one place long enough to be still with your feelings and thoughts? All of these disguised expressions or distractions can mask what is really bothering you.

## Masks Can Hurt as They Protect

Other forms can be more obvious attempts to turn back the clock. Been wearing down those track shoes? You might relate to Victoria, who was using excessive exercise to mask her feelings about her changing looks and aging, literally running away. She learned in a painful way the limitations of trying to stretch the limits.

Victoria, ordinarily active and full of energy, was feeling exhausted and more down than usual. At 50, she decided running a marathon was a good goal to work toward. *"I've always raced,"* she explained, *"but nothing this big. I got the idea after a jog with some of my younger running friends. I was changing at the gym and felt unusually tired and old. I decided training for a marathon might lift my spirits."* Asking Victoria why this felt important to her now (thinking this might be her uh-oh moment), she said, *"I had raced half-marathons throughout my 20s and 30s and it was a great feeling to be in such good shape. I also had my best love affairs then and I'm sure it had to do with how good I looked. I just feel it's a good idea to challenge myself this way."*

Unfortunately, Victoria developed shin splints while training. She tried to run through the pain, but stopped when even walking became unbearable. She dropped her marathon plan and with it her spirits dropped too. As she focused on her sadness, she realized she was more upset about the lost version of her self than the lost marathon. She was frightened about the changes she saw in her face and body and realized those were what she was really running from. Gradually, Victoria learned to accept her changing—yet still very fit—appearance and began to enjoy a new definition of beauty. Awareness about what lay behind her mask was her first step.

Make no mistake, we often encourage women to take action, rather than remain passive victims. But activity must be accompanied by thought and understanding. Some actions that appear to help women defy age can actually victimize us instead. For example working out excessively is a culturally sanctioned and simplistic approach to the complicated issues facing aging. Taking action—even if compulsive—may appear to be in keeping with the modern image of proactive women. But too often the action is directed against a target that is unclear, not to mention endlessly moving. It keeps women like Victoria locked in a battle against the enemy, but one we can never win. We remain chained to an image of the past, focused on what we felt and looked like. We are holding onto an illusion.

As trained therapists, we respect the need for the comfort provided by masks. They are akin to the kind of coping measures people use to deal with emotional difficulties in general, unrelated to aging and beauty. For example, when we are presented with news of a loved one's death, we respond, *"It's not true. I can't believe it,"* expressing temporary denial that allows the full reality to soak in more slowly. When we hear about a threatening world event, our natural protective reaction is to convince ourselves it couldn't happen where we live. When we are jilted by a boyfriend, we convince ourselves he was a jerk and that we're better off without him. These are natural coping measures.

Such reactions to visible signs of aging—though comforting for the moment—can disconnect us from the source of our discomfort and lead to complications. Sometimes these reactions can even be self-destructive, as was the case for Janet.

Janet, a widow, had lost her husband to colon cancer four years ago, when she was 56. During his illness, she felt like she aged about ten years. Now that she was 60, she felt a strong urge to move on. She told us, *"I decided I needed to pull my act together, sold my house in the suburbs, and luckily got a part-time job as a receptionist. I just wanted to leave everything behind."* It seemed like a natural reaction to the desire to let go of her past, the sadness about her husband, and the wish to create a new life. But as we asked further, we realized that changes she saw on her face and body also provoked impulsivity. Janet took her husband's life insurance and some of the money she had saved for retirement to buy an overpriced apartment and scheduled a tummy tuck and face-lift. She had only one consultation with a doctor *"who didn't charge as much as others."* She wanted it done quickly and didn't want to think about it much. There were some complications with her surgery, infections that led to repeated surgical procedures to correct the problem. Unfortunately, she was also dissatisfied with the results, especially how her face looked after it was done. Although she had hoped for a new start, she felt she felt she didn't recognize herself. She fell into a deep depression, confused about whether her sadness was about her face, the loss of her husband, or the losses she felt about getting older in general.

When women like Janet reach for relief from discomfort, without using accumulated wisdom and experience, the solutions are rarely long-lasting. While Janet's instinctive reactions to relocate homes and surgically improve her looks may have distracted her temporarily, they also served to disconnect her from her feelings. Although Janet's husband had died four years ago, we felt she first needed to fully mourn his loss before she could make thoughtful, long-term plans for her future.

*   *   *

**Reversing the results of surgical procedures is usually not an option. Women therefore need to think long and hard to determine if these tucks and lifts are in fact externally managing feelings that need to be dealt with internally.**

. . .

*"One of the painful aspects of life today is that women are encouraged to turn to quite dramatic cosmetic procedures in the face of loss,"* says author Susie Orbach. As a therapist to many public figures, supposedly Princess Diana among them, Orbach is no doubt aware that masks can provide temporary relief to inner struggles. But by clouding the issue at hand, they actually make the future more difficult to manage and can often lead to greater confusion. The key is to gradually expose the feelings behind our masks, allowing better access to the ambivalence we have about beauty. If we respect and value the complexity of these emotions, they will emerge with less panic or shame. Actress Cate Blanchett, known for disappearing behind cinematic masks, taps into what is likely the fundamental fear facing us all when she says, *"We're all fearful of death, let's not kid ourselves. I'm simply not panicking, as my laugh lines grow deeper. Who wants a face with no history, no sense of humor?"*

Once we recognize the behavioral and emotional forms our masks take, the more options we will have to develop new strategies for dealing with our changing looks. It's time to move inward, from the measures that prevent us from awareness to the words that tell us what we are really thinking and feeling about our changing appearance. They are our internal dialogues. If we learn to listen carefully, we can move on.

## Identify and Look Behind
## Your Masks

▶ Are you behaving out of character?

▶ Do you find yourself obsessed with some activity and can't let go?

▶ Are you ruminating about an idea, even if it seems irrelevant to your life?

▶ Do you find yourself unusually preoccupied by physical discomforts? Worried about your child's health or your parent's aging?

▶ Try to connect any of the above thoughts or behaviors to your changing looks and uncover the underlying emotions you may have about aging.

# chapter five

* * *

## Internal Dialogues

*Women have this ongoing internal voice.
They'll look in the mirror and say, "Oh, you fat cow!"
If someone walked up to you and said, "Hi, you fat
cow," you would not accept that. So why would you
accept that from yourself?*

— Victoria Principal

## Step Three: Opening Up

In the last chapter we identified the masks we wear, though we don't always *see* them. Now we move on to the internal dialogues we hear, though we don't always *listen* to them. Internal dialogues are running commentaries playing inside our heads that relate to how we see ourselves and how we believe others see us. One very accomplished and usually wise 52-year-old woman told us, *"Lately, I find while talking to other women, I have a conversation with myself, like 'I know she's thinking I look old, that I am aging badly, as badly as she is. I can see it in her eyes. I hear her thoughts in my head.' It's Woody Allen–like, you know, as if I am having two dialogues at once, only this is a script I'm not enjoying!"*

While masks serve to protect, internal dialogues serve to expose. Although they are part of everyone's natural interior life, dialogues about our looks intensify as women begin the aging process. For some women, these dialogues can stay outside of our awareness, hardly noticeable. For others, they play like a broken record, persistent and repetitive. The meaning and value of internal dialogues for most women remain unclear until spoken out loud. When we verbalize them, we discover how often the words and feelings focus on how we look, how we don't want to look, and how we wish we looked.

◦ ◦ ◦

**Step Three teaches us to use internal dialogues to open the window to our inner psychological experience. As we shed the protective gear and face our honest emotions, we have an opportunity to understand what is really going on behind our masks.**

◦ ◦ ◦

Internal dialogues can be "switched on" in any number of ways and in any number of places. It may be on your way to work, a glance in a mirror, a look in the eyes of another. They can be positive in nature—one woman, who saw herself in a storefront reflection on her way to work, heard these words in her head, *"I'm glad I wore this outfit since my whole staff is meeting today."* But more often the tone is judgmental, less supportive or self-congratulatory. Another woman saw herself in an elevator mirror, and during the 20-floor ride down from her apartment she thought, *"Ugh, my roots are showing. I hate to go out like this . . . I'll go back to get a hat."* Still another, as she glanced at her image reflected in the glass bookshelves in her classroom said, *"I should remember to stand up straight. I look like one of those hunched-over old teachers kids make fun of."* Some women tell us they try to avoid reflections altogether if they can so as not to hear their internal dialogues. As one summed up, *"Why should I see what other people see? It only depresses me."* Sound familiar?

Sometimes the content of internal dialogues echo distorted conclusions we draw about ourselves. In childhood, we create stories to make sense of the world when it confuses us, like when we conclude, *"Daddy must have left Mommy because I was a bad girl,"* or, *"Mommy loves my sister more because she's prettier than I am."* As adults, our internal dialogues continue to create stories to help us make sense of the world.

In our internal dialogues, we often ascribe roles, motives and meaning to the behavior of others. For example, Gail, a designer, says, *"My husband thinks I'm unattractive. That's why he watches so much TV,"* when in actuality it is Gail herself who feels unattractive, but assumes these are the thoughts her husband shares. Another woman, Andrea, who hosts a political talk show, typically hears words in her head like, *"Everyone is staring at the dark circles under my eyes."* In spite of harsh criticism typically hurled toward female public figures as they age, the fact is that Andrea's audience adores her and is focused more on what she has to say than how she looks saying it. What Andrea was doing is not uncommon. There are dialogues we hold with ourselves that attempt to rationalize why we feel the way we do, even if they're not based on real facts.

When our internal dialogues are carefully examined, instead of being taken on face value, they reveal our own genuine feelings about our appearance. We have to look closely because they can be disguised behind other distracting reactions. One woman, who openly opposed her friend's preoccupation with age-defying cosmetics and often criticized the use of Botox and fillers, revealed that her own internal dialogues included, *"Maybe there is something to these treatments. They scare me, but I'm feeling if I don't give these things a try, I'll be the only one left with an old wrinkled face."* Sound familiar?

## Listening to the Words Inside Our Heads

Listening carefully to our own internal conversations offers important insights into the way we feel about ourselves. What do you hear when you listen to Melinda's private thoughts?

Melinda's internal dialogues were revealed when she responded to being asked to participate in a college friend's 60th birthday video. At first she said, *"Sure, I'd be glad to. I'm flattered."* She and five other women in their 50s were asked to tell stories about the birthday boy. As the date neared, Melinda's thoughts volleyed in her head like a play by play of the U.S. Open. *"I wonder who else will be in it. I know Jane will be and she looks so young and Sally is in such great shape. Some people haven't seen me in years and I'm scared what they'll think now . . . Maybe I'll make sure there are no close-ups or profiles, though I know that's so vain. I am not going to watch it when it comes up because I know I'll be depressed the rest of the party."*

Jealousy? Insecurity? Competition? As Melinda paid attention to her internal dialogues, she recognized that behind her initial laissez-faire attitude about the party project lay a great deal of insecurity and self-criticism about her aging looks. The words she heard inside her head revealed that the battle Melinda waged was one she knew she couldn't win. She was competing with other women, trying to physically replicate who she thought she used to be. When we explained this to her, she said she had always compared herself to others, even when she was younger, never feeling satisfied with her own face and body. We reminded her that her struggles now seemed like intensified versions of old familiar ones and that perhaps she would be more successful if she realized her difficulties were *within* herself rather than between herself and others.

Sometimes, as therapists, we're asked about the value of working with our internal dialogues or the benefit of saying them out loud. *"It's bad enough I think these thoughts, why should I speak them?"* women often ask. The answer lies in a fundamental psychological principle: keeping thoughts hidden—heard only by you—can give them more power. Bringing them to the surface of our consciousness weakens their hold and allows us to use awareness for insight and change. In most forms of psychotherapy, change results from awareness and increased clarity, which ultimately leads to choice and greater emotional freedom. Unfortunately, we're not always aware that we are unaware.

What we do know is that these repetitive conversations are often almost imperceptible, much the way background noise goes unnoticed. We encourage you to listen carefully to them, because even if the words have seemed unimportant and irrelevant up until now, they hold significance as your appearance changes. As you read the dialogues in this section and the sample ones written throughout this chapter, we hope you'll reflect upon your own dialogues and connect them to your personal experience of beauty. This cognitive tool can help our wise and accomplished generation gain control over these fruitless, repetitive conversations that leave us feeling stuck, going nowhere.

## Moving Further Inward

At this point in your progression from the external to the internal, we remind you that it's important to move slowly and gradually. When we work with patients, we don't just reach behind their masks, yank them off, and expose their inner emotional experience. We recognize that layers of protection evolve for personal and cultural reasons and we respect their role in psychological development. Like the sensitive skin beneath a scab, bringing internal dialogues into the open exposes vulnerability and discomfort and is a process that takes time. It also takes trust.

Just as a patient needs to have faith in the psychotherapeutic process, borrowed confidence is required to uncover internal dialogues. It means trusting that even if you feel awkward, embarrassed, or dismissive about your thoughts—perhaps even about the very idea of beauty—the process of bringing these inner ramblings to the surface will be worth it. Acknowledging your internal dialogues depends on your tolerance for examining your feelings and the confidence that in doing so, your ideas about beauty will get clarified and your perceptions of yourself will become more grounded in reality.

Think free association—thoughts that flow uncensored in our minds. Think dreams—images that emerge during sleep. As you might know, both are tools used by some therapists to hone in on underlying meanings behind our thoughts and feelings. With internal dialogues too, therapists work to liberate ideas from inside women's heads so they can be useful toward understanding their meaning. We tell women to listen not only to the words of inner dialogues, but to the emotional tone the words convey. The process of exposing these thoughts, unencumbered and uncensored, allows present day ideas and feelings, once embedded in a vague context, to become connected to a very personal one. Knowledge of the content and source of emotions allows for a greater sense of control and the possibility of change.

Rosie, 58, said she used to hear the words *fatty pants* over and over in her head when she was a teen. The phrase was started long ago by Billy, the younger of her two brothers, but both of them taunted her well into her adult life. She reacted sensitively as she got older, anytime anyone looked her way. Now, as she walked into a room of strangers, she often imagined words like *fat old slob,* in the minds of others. The content of the taunts shifted, but the tone and critical attitude remained the same. No matter how Rosie tried to care for herself, she couldn't stop the running commentaries. They were so second nature she barely noticed them until we asked her to say them out loud. *"I'm actually in better shape now than I've ever been, but it's hard to shake a perception I've lived with all my life. I guess it helps to be reminded that the world is not filled with people who think like my brothers!"*

Everyone's story is different. Rosie's perception of herself was caught amid constant taunting by her siblings. There are themes among women that begin to emerge and make sense when spoken out loud and shared. They are not random, although they may seem to be. Our dialogues have roots in our personal lives and in our particular culture. In this journey, we know the general path, but internal dialogues will help you find your own personal route.

## Why Are We So Hard on Ourselves?

Interestingly, we find that women's internal dialogues tend to be harsher and more judgmental than the real exchanges they have with others. Given how closely our culture equates youth with beauty, women inwardly admonish themselves for failing to live up to this unrealistic equation. Studies show that the tendency for self-criticism in girls begins as early as age 10 or 11 and is focused primarily on their bodies, faces and weight. This tendency intensifies throughout adolescence, slows down during adulthood, but shows up again more strongly in the internal dialogues of women at midlife.

**INTERNAL DIALOGUE #1**

• • •

I'm feeling blah.

I look blah. I don't feel like myself.

My skin looks lackluster.

Is that gray in my hair or a blond streak?

It's gray.

Where'd that come from?

I'm getting old.

How can that be? I'm only 41.

My god, I am 41!

I was just in my 30s.

I'm too young for gray.

My mother had gray hair.

I guess I'll have to color it like she did.

I'll go out for a run.

If I do six miles today, I'll feel better.

I can't run six, my knees hurt.

I'm so tired.

But that's what makes me feel better.

I don't know what I'm going to do.

I'm feeling so blah.

Many women feel aging is their fault. We blame ourselves for a natural process, ashamed and embarrassed about our "failure." We feel deserving of the internal criticism yet feel angered that we can't escape the scolding. Just when we need a little praise and support during a difficult phase of our lives, we are harder than ever on ourselves. Something is wrong with this picture, frame, and focus.

Sally clearly missed opportunities to see herself as others did. She couldn't even enjoy the applause.

There were more than a hundred women cheering as Sally got down from the podium after giving a lecture. She was a confident public speaker, having given speeches for 30 years. But today, after sweating through her clothes from intermittent, strong hot flashes, she thought, *"that was hard to get through . . . a real performance . . . I felt like fanning myself, but I can just imagine what people would have thought . . . I've always sweated a lot, but this is different . . . I felt like a furnace and the last thing I wanted was to call attention to the wet spots creeping on my blouse. This menopause thing sucks.*

*I'm calmer than ever when I speak, but definitely not cool and collected! I must have looked like a wreck up there."*

In spite of the confidence Sally should have been feeling, her internal dialogues exposed the embarrassment and insecurity she suffered over a normal fact of life. What a shame these natural biological realities have turned into sources of humiliation, much the way menstruation was once perceived as embarrassing to adolescents. Sally's competence far exceeded the noisy goings-on inside her head.

## INTERNAL DIALOGUE #2

• • •

I had a huge dinner, but I feel like eating.

May be I'll just have a little bit of ice cream.

But I want to wear my jeans tomorrow. And they're tight as it is.

Jack used to like the way I look in them.

Jack doesn't seem that interested in me lately.

He's staying at work longer these days.

His new associate is so gorgeous.

She must be in her 30s.

When we were in our 30s, Jack wanted to have sex more.

Maybe I should have liposuction.

My stomach has rolls of fat. How can I compete?

I can't believe I ate the whole pint of ice cream.

I feel disgusting.

Angeline was seen by many as a beautiful middle-aged woman—but this was not how she felt on the inside. Like Sally, her inner dialogues revealed old wounds, and new ones that were often self-inflicted.

Former fashion model Angeline, now a photographer at 39, often had conversations in the bathroom with her magnified mirror. While examining her face, she thought, *"I used to look at myself close up all the time, no problem. Sure, I was critical when I was modeling, but it was about my makeup, or my complexion or hairstyle. Now, I want to scream about my whole face! How could this happen to me? My face looks like it's been through hell and headed for worse . . . maybe it was years of caked-on makeup or all the late nights out drinking in my heyday . . . why didn't I take better care of myself? I can't believe what I see . . . these lines . . . out of nowhere . . . under my eyes, these flaps of extra skin drive me crazy . . . I can't look. I'm disgusting. I've got to do something. But I can't afford surgery . . . I should have done something when I was making a ton of money . . . I should have known what was coming."* She focused on the younger girls and too often compared herself to them. *"I can't even remember having a face like theirs and it's sad I didn't appreciate what I had then,"* she thought.

Sometimes the source of harsh, critical dialogues lies not in unreachable cultural standards, but in figures from our personal history. Internal dialogues can help us recognize where the voices come from and the role they play in the development of our self-image.

Eva, 45 was visiting her in-laws with her husband. Matt often reminded her that his mom rarely had a kind thing to say to anyone and Eva dreaded their visits. Before they even walked in the door, Eva said to herself, *"I know Matt's mom will pull him aside and say I'm a mess. He is their prince and I'm the ugly duckling he got stuck with . . . I never can please her . . . last time she told me I should see her dermatologist. I don't have time to do what she does . . . manicures and facials . . . I'm*

*consumed caring for our three children, her grandchildren
for God's sake! I guess I could have put on makeup . . .
I hope she doesn't insult me. I'll be so angry. I used to
have screaming fights with my mom and dad about how
I looked. That's why I don't visit them anymore. I feel so
bad. Maybe Matt's mom is right. I am a mess."*

In spite of being a successful teacher and mother, the voices
Eva heard in her head made her feel like a "mess." Listening
carefully to her internal dialogues, and paying attention to
their source, helped Eva understand why she felt so reactive to
her mother-in-law's attitude. On the one hand, she resented her
mother-in-law's emphasis on looks and intellectually believed
her husband's warnings about his mom's nonpartisan criticism. Yet Eva couldn't help herself from caring about what her
mother-in-law thought and kept trying hard to please her. And
something personal was resonating.

By exploring even further, we learned that Eva's mother
had been unhappy with her own appearance and had displayed
chronic disappointment in Eva's lack of attention to her looks.
Eva had been and still was interested in things other than
beauty. Recalling former family relationships, via internal dialogues, helped Eva gain perspective on the feelings these visits
with her mother-in-law engendered.

We use internal dialogues to reveal not only the cast of
characters that play a role in our self-image, but the influence
these people have on its development. Once you let the dialogues flow, voices that may have been disguised or only mildly
recognizable, become clearer. And as you identify them, you
will be better equipped to manage them.

### INTERNAL DIALOGUE #3

• • •

I should sample that new cream I saw on TV.
It works from underneath the skin, rejuvenating
they said. I could use that.

These mirrors. They're so magnified!

I can see everything. It's frightening. I hate
what I'm seeing.

Everything is falling. My eyelids. Even my neck. What
are these spots?

Nobody at our Christmas party paid any
attention to me.

My body is okay. It's my face.

I don't have any spunk.

Maybe I should go to the nutrition center and
pick up some vitamins.

What were those herbal supplements I read
in *Vogue* that can make your skin look better?

I have no room for any more pills in my
medicine cabinet.

I should throw some out and replace them.

I wonder if people notice how old I feel.

I wonder if I'll ever meet anyone.

Maybe my time has run out.

Oh, god help me.

Who can help me?

It's just going to get worse.

I have no future.

I am going to get left behind and be alone.

Forty-five-year-old Hannah is married, works as a real estate agent, and has a 12-year-old son, Ben. She often went to yoga before work and as she was getting ready to go one day she heard words in her head, *"I'm feeling blah . . . I don't really feel like going to yoga today . . . I'm so unmotivated recently . . . yoga just isn't doing it for me lately . . . It forces me to look in the mirror and I don't see anything I can feel good about . . . why do they have mirrors in these places, anyhow? . . . I think it's time for me to stop going. What's the use? . . . What's the use of doing anything when everything I do doesn't get better . . . everything seems to go downhill . . . my body . . . my work . . . I'm 45 . . . what will happen when I'm 55 . . . why am I thinking this way? I used to be such an upbeat person . . . must be hormones . . . Ben says I'm a downer. That's probably why he'd rather spend time with his friends than me . . . I don't blame him. I'm so dull. I look dull, my skin is so lackluster. I'm lacking something, everything . . ."*

Hannah told us this dialogue was being played over and over in her head. She knew she was depressed, and the focus kept going back to her body and face. We asked her to listen to the words carefully to see if she could hear the themes. As she opened up more, Hannah recognized her dialogues sounded very much the way her father used to talk about himself. After a serious cycling accident in his 40s, Hannah's dad walked with a cane and grew increasingly resentful about his disability. From Hannah's perspective, her dad was a grumpy old man as long as she could remember.

Hearing her own internal dialogues enabled Hannah to make the connection between her thoughts and her father's attitude and behavior. What she heard in herself was actually what she felt from him—anger, resentment, and resignation. Recognizing this association to her father enabled Hannah to look at herself more objectively. It helped her understand why she had anticipated midlife changes with feeling of sadness. As she connected the dots, she was able to begin separating the despair her father's accident generated and what she could be feeling at this point in her life.

While Hannah's dialogues sparked memories of Dad, Sheila's reminded her of how her looks had been tied to lifelong issues with her twin sister.

> Sheila is a single woman in her 40s whose internal dialogues were hard to ignore as she took her lunch break at Bloomingdale's. Not the shopping type, she surreptitiously scoped out the cosmetic counters, avoiding the saleswomen approaching her to sample

items. *"I hate shopping . . . this is the last place I want to spend my time, but I saw an ad in a magazine I was reading at my doctor's office . . . said something about evening out the dark spots on skin. I know about false advertising, but this product was made by a dermatologist. And these spots annoy me. My twin sister had hers surgically removed, some laser process. I'd never have surgery . . . goes against everything I believe . . . but I can't stop noticing how my skin is changing . . . I look like someone I don't know . . . I always thought I looked younger than my sister . . . but she's taken care of her skin with all sorts of creams . . . maybe I should too . . . but then I'll be as silly as her . . . wasting my money and time . . . I'm embarrassed at how I look these days. My sister and I used to laugh when people asked if she was older, because I was, by a minute. Now I look ten years older. What happened?"*

Even women who are surprised to be having internal dialogues about changing looks can learn from them. Sheila realized she was conflicted about paying attention to beauty issues. Its low priority in her life had once helped distinguish her from her twin. This dynamic was revived in midlife and revealed itself in her internal dialogues. Sheila began to realize that she no longer had to differentiate herself from her sister by being dismissive of her looks and that she was doing herself a disservice in remaining neglectful of them.

## How to Use Your Internal Dialogues

Like the women above, you can use your internal dialogues to understand your perception of yourself and break free from paralyzing reactions to changing looks. Even if your dialogues are barely audible and not easily accessible, listen carefully for the insight they provide.

Maggie knew she was unhappy, and her inner dialogues could only be described as circuitous. Until pressed and supported, she never imagined her inner thoughts could be so revelatory.

A 48-year-old hairdresser, Maggie told us she just wasn't feeling very good about herself. She said, *"I am tired a lot, a bit down, and don't know why."* Confused and unaware where to start, she said, *"I avoid looking at myself in the mirror, especially when I style my clients' hair."* When asked why, she said, *"It just makes me feel uncomfortable and bad."* We suggested she look just this one time and take note of what she heard in her head. We told her that her internal dialogues would help clarify what she was feeling. This is what she heard. *"I have eight clients today . . . I look tired . . . I should have fixed myself up this morning. I don't bother these days. It just makes me feel worse. I wonder if people see what I see? Who would want their hair done by someone like me? Where did these puffy circles under my eyes come from? I remember my mother used to use cold packs on hers . . . I look like her. When did that happen? My husband doesn't seem to notice, but I don't know what to make of that . . . because we haven't had sex in a while. Why is Brian at his computer all the time? I wonder if he's looking at porn. I've got to do something about this face."*

The first step for women is to find the courage to look inside and listen. For Maggie, once she did, her dialogues provided clues to her fatigue and depression. She sensed hopelessness, not certain of any solution to her discomfort. But her reality, as is true for many women, was actually more manageable than her fears. When Maggie let herself listen to her own thoughts, even she knew they seemed unrealistic and distorted. For example, when asked if it was likely that her husband was disinterested in her, she admitted it was unlikely, since, *"he always tells me he loves me. I think it's me, not him that I question. I'm not sure I should really do anything to my face until I talk to him about it."* She told us she realized her clients were actually quite devoted to her, as her husband was, and that neither likely saw her as unattractive as she did. We talked about other traits that people clearly appreciated and asked Maggie to think about how she might be able to practice some self-appreciation.

We see that when Maggie was willing to look and listen, she could take the next step—learning what feelings she had been avoiding and why. Maggie's fear was focused largely on becoming like her mom, who had given up on herself years ago. Maggie learned how to use this insight to reframe the lens through which she saw herself and rewrite the content of her dialogues. By doing so, she could rewrite a future that included looking after herself, less out of fear and more out of the desire to feel better.

Many women are not nearly so aware of an inner life as Maggie learned to be. They may initially resist listening to their internal dialogues or connecting to their feelings. But as therapists, we try to tackle that resistance in an attempt to have women come to a better understanding of themselves. We hone in on why there may be avoidance of the very thoughts worth exploring.

Annie, a 55-year-old waitress, divorced with two kids, told us she never had conversations with herself about her looks. She said, *"People who are so focused on their looks are too preoccupied with themselves."* We understood her point of view, but asked her to imagine herself in front of a mirror and tell us what came to mind. She said, *"nothing . . . nothing comes to mind."* With prompting, we asked her to try to let her imagination go, as if she was preparing to go out with a new man she had met. She said, with some irritation, *"Okay, I feel stupid doing this, but, okay . . . I look terrible. I haven't looked good since before having my twins . . . I'm not worth looking at, although I once thought I was cute . . . and this is definitely not worth talking about."*

There are plenty of women like Annie, who express a lack of interest, almost disdain, for their appearance. However, Annie's dialogues revealed that her indifference concealed a negative attitude about her self-image. It's one thing to have minimal interest in one's appearance or to choose to relegate it to an unimportant role in life and another to feel the need to belittle the whole issue. Annie seemed to actively suspend caring for herself once her children were born. We encouraged her to listen to her internal dialogues and to the tone that we so clearly heard.

We knew that if Annie listened more closely to her words, and questioned what else might have been contributing to her disregard for her appearance, she could use her internal dialogues to free herself to make actual choices about caring—or not—about her looks. With some coaxing, Annie told us the story about what happened after her twins were born. The clue to her bitterness came when she shared the memory of having walked in on her husband having an affair with a good friend, a woman 20 years younger, while pregnant with her twins. She received sole custody of her children, and took them miles away to live with her mother, where she still resides today. Her mother had been living alone, after Annie's stepfather had walked out on her mom five years earlier, so she had been glad to have the company. As Annie became more open about this difficult time, she acknowledged there was greater meaning to her dismissal of her looks than she first could admit.

She learned that what lay behind her mask of indifference was not just resignation. Annie felt deeply hurt by her husband's infidelity and betrayed by her friend. Consumed by anger over their deception, it was difficult for Annie to access her sadness and mourn the loss of her marriage, feeling only resignation instead. These emotions also resonated with similar ones her mother had shared with Annie about men in general. *"Men are just bad news,"* her mom had told Annie as far back as she could remember. Annie said, *"and now I know what she means."*

You hardly need be a therapist to see that Annie's apathy and negativity about her self-image was fueled by misdirected anger about her failed marriage—anger she not only felt toward the father of her children, but to the men in her mother's life as well. We often find that when we are unaware of the origins of our present day behavior, we unwittingly act in self-destructive ways.

Next, we move on to uncover the roots of our internal dialogues. These are the developmental seeds of our self-image—the who, what, where, when, and why of how we came to see our selves as we do. These roots are embedded in our family history, and uncovering them will help us understand how our self-image undergoes change as we age.

## Listening to Your Internal Dialogues

▶ Take note of the words that come to mind—as you get dressed in the morning, look in the mirror, walk down the street, wash your makeup off, get into bed with your mate—and write them down.

▶ Do these words remind you of anyone? Do you hear your mother talking to you? Your father talking to you mother? A sibling?

▶ See if you can use these dialogues to clarify where these feelings originate and what they are truly about.

▶ Try rewriting your dialogues with a more gentle, kinder tone, the way you might talk to a friend you care about. Instead of *"you look so tired and dreadful today,"* shift the tone to something like, *"I wonder if staying up so late last night makes it hard to look and feel energetic today."* Replace the self-critical *you* with the self-assertive *I*. Practice by replaying these new dialogues over in your head until they become your new ones.

# chapter six

* * *

## What Do Moms Have to Do with It?

*A mother who radiates self-love and
self-acceptance actually vaccinates her
daughter against low self-esteem.*

— Naomi Wolf

### Step Four: Going Back in Time

Poor Mom. Why does she always end up on the psychological hot seat? Sigmund Freud analyzed her. Eminen rapped about her. Faye Dunaway portrayed her with a wire hanger in hand. Let's face it: mothers are the go-to figures in songs, stories, and screenplays for a reason. She is at the heart of Step Four: returning to our roots to understand the significant role our mothers—and others—play in the experience of our changing looks.

In the previous chapter, we identified the cast of characters reflected in our internal dialogues and found that Mom often played a starring role. Wasn't that her voice reminding you to stand up straight, asking if you *really* planned to wear those pants? Wasn't that her reminding you at the dinner table, *"There are kids starving in China, so eat,"* only to be followed by, *"do you really need that dessert?"* For some of us, being made aware of these dialogues is the first time we recognize that our innermost thoughts, and ultimately our self-image, have a great deal to do with those who reared us. Remember Eva? She was the woman who anticipated criticism prior to every visit with her mother-in-law and recognized that her internal dialogues resonated with critical comments heard throughout her childhood. Or Rosie, who learned that the taunts she heard in her head today were similar to ones used by her siblings while growing up.

While occasionally those who reared us were our fathers, grandparents, aunts, or even siblings, most often it is Mom whom we recall. Not only did her attitude about beauty influence the development of our self-image, but she is also our physical example of aging. Both internally and externally— from our bone structure to our blood type, from our coloring to our mannerisms—we are genetically programmed to be most similar to our biological mother. By nature, our own aging process parallels hers more than anyone else's. For some, this is not only all right, but a source of comfort. But for many of us, this fact is less heartening. As teenagers, we may have said, *"She seems so old!"* These days it may be, *"She is so old,"* followed by the ultimate recognition, *"I have become my mother!"*

We learned in previous chapters that masking our emotional reactions to the aging process leaves us confused by what we feel. We are similarly resistant to recognizing the never-ending bond between mother and daughter. Author Victoria Secunda writes: *"Mothers are their daughters' role model, their biological and emotional road map, the arbiter of all their relationships."* Our mothers may carry us for nine months, but we carry them with us throughout our lives, fostering a powerful identification and connection. Understandably, you may not be eager to dwell on whatever your particular relationship has been or how your mother's present may predict your future. Yet this is what we encourage you to do in Step Four.

•  •  •

**The failure to look clearly at the natural continuity between mother and daughter unwittingly leads you to have life experiences that will likely parallel hers, whether you**

choose to or not. Step Four will provide you with a way to view your mother-daughter relationship—both emotionally and physically—so you understand it, rather than feel victimized by it.

● ● ●

## Our Very First Mirror

Let's begin at the beginning. Observational studies suggest that perceptions of our self-image originate even before we can speak. Our very first glimpse of ourselves is likely found in the mirror of our mother's eyes during infancy. In her glances and later through her words and behaviors—how we were touched, held, and caressed—we begin to develop a psychological and physical image of ourselves. These experiences become intertwined, creating a foundation for a conception of who we are that is believed to be well underway by age three or four.

At best, a strong and appealing self-image starts when love is reflected back at us in the gleam of our mother's eyes. If those eyes are filled with unconditional approval and affection, mother and child both bask in immense pleasure, experiencing themselves as blissfully beautiful. It is in this mutual glow that the earliest seeds of positive self-esteem are planted.

Psychologists contend that this positive feeling starts not only in the loving glances mirrored back from Mother's eye, but in our ability to feel comforted and comfortable with the caretaker in that important role. For example, if the caretaker has a positive regard for herself—one that conveys and encourages individuality and self-acceptance—her child will follow suit. As infants, and even into adulthood, we yearn to identify with the caretakers who provide security and strength. We see them as role models and internalize aspects of who they are into our own sense of self.

Although you are not likely to recall these early memories, try asking yourself questions like, *"If I think back to childhood, what do I imagine I'd see in the eyes of my mother as she looked at me? Adoration? Pride? Disappointment? Jealousy? Aversion? And how did Mom view herself? Did Dad look at her with pleasure?"* Do any memories remind you of how you look at yourself today?

Girls who experience early positive interchanges in their relationships most often become women who go forward into adulthood with a strong self-image. Regardless of one's physical features, this sturdiness provides a cushion against the complicated messages culture throws in our way. These girls grow up to be women whose internal perception is less likely to undergo radical swings as aging occurs.

Remember Felice? She was the woman who had gone to her gynecologist for a routine visit, but ended up hearing unsolicited suggestions about plastic surgery. We were curious about Felice's capacity to remain secure about her appearance in the face of her doctor's comments implying otherwise. As we interviewed her, it became clear that in more ways than her appearance, she had a robustness and flexibility to her sense of self and that this confidence was rooted in her family history. *"My mom and dad always made me feel I was the most wonderful girl in their world. Since I was their only daughter, with three brothers, I felt special being the girl. I knew I was adored. Although I was nothing great to look at . . . big nose, pretty chunky, I grew up thinking I looked okay. But they made me feel beautiful. It wasn't about my looks. I was just the apple of their eye."*

Of course, many girls grow up differently than Felice did, feeling less secure and admired, even if they have physical features that might invite adoration. No matter how beautiful a child may or may not be, a caretaker can respond not with love, but a number of other feelings which can be reflected in a child's first mirror: indifference, jealousy, and antagonism, for example. Some parents, who yearn for affirmation themselves, invest in their daughters' looks to compensate for their own lack of confidence, though the results are often dissatisfying to both. Mothers may adore and adorn their daughters, trying to give them what they never received, embarking on a vicarious voyage. Sometimes we see this in mothers who dress daughters as "mini me's" or worse, compete with them.

Judith had been a blond, blue-eyed angelic-looking little girl, who grew up with pictures of herself plastered all over her mother's home. She told us that when she sees those pictures now, at age 51, she has little memory of ever looking that way. *"My mom brought me up by herself and was devoted to me."* Judith's mom had been an overweight and unkempt woman most of her life. *"She loved to dress me up, with colorful bows in my hair. She even let me wear makeup sometimes as a kid. She got me to do some modeling, but I didn't like it and I think I disappointed her when I didn't get much work. I did a couple of ads and one small part in a low-budget film. It made her so happy, but by the time I was 13, I had bad acne. I never was cute again. I drank during my teens. I gained a lot of weight. My mom is a full-blown alcoholic now and I haven't spoken to her in years."* Judith says although she only has vague memories of her youth, mostly from pictures, she clearly remembers that she never felt pretty, even when her mom was so eager to have others think that way about her.

When adult-child relationships are dominated by the needs of the parent, girls may come to feel their looks are essential to the satisfaction they provide that parent. Surely, Judith felt that way. Looking good may have been extremely important to her mother, but like a pretty dress that can be taken on or off, this positive feeling is ephemeral, thus not an asset Judith could experience within. When girls like Judith grow up, it becomes difficult for them to accept that they are beautiful because they never felt truly valued for who they were. Their beauty, usurped by their parents' needs, leaves these girls to associate their looks with mixed emotions at best.

These are the women who develop a shaky sense of themselves and an unstable internal experience of how they look. When their looks change, they are left trying desperately to hold on to an illusory self-image they associate with a vague sense of having been loved. Their attempts to recapture rose-tinted memories—of times when they equated beauty with attention—are tainted by disappointment and frustration. These are also the women most likely to fall victim to our culture's paradoxical messages that tell us beauty matters, but it doesn't. They assume beauty brings happiness, but they are left dissatisfied and disillusioned. In the end, these women fail to feel attractive regardless of how good they look or how attractive others perceive them to be.

Some parents devalue their children simply because they are female and this feeling too can be reflected in the child's first mirror. From the moment we are conceived, the relationship our mother and father have to us is based, at least in part, on gender. Despite our cultural advances, the idea of conceiving a girl is still often considered second to having a boy—in some cultures more so than others, and in some families more so than others. Unfortunately and unfairly, these attitudes can become internalized from early infancy on, often without conscious awareness, leading to low self-esteem.

Karen, a 52-year-old occupational therapist, reported that she feared that her husband wasn't finding her attractive. *"I'm not sure I ever understood why my husband fell in love with me, but recently I feel he's falling out of love."* She said she didn't have any real evidence of this change, but was convinced something was different. To get his attention, she went on a radical diet, lost 25 pounds and then underwent several cosmetic procedures thinking it was her looks that had changed their relationship. When we asked her what made her conclude this, she told us, *"I just feel lost when it comes to my looks and figured everyone else was doing surgery, so maybe I should."* It became clear as she talked about her history that Karen's mother had given her no introduction to the rituals of being a woman, nor did they share any pleasurable activities typically associated with femininity. *"My mom never showed me how to put on makeup. I have no memory of her fussing with my hair or taking me shopping . . . not even for my prom dress. To tell you the truth, I can't recall my mom ever doing those things for herself either. I really don't think she liked being a woman."*

Karen had few childhood experiences that would have allowed her to feel her femininity was valued and special. As an adult, external measures like dieting and surgery were ineffective in relieving her insecurity. Nor did they lead her to enjoy the pleasure her husband derived from her looks. Karen was unable to feel attractive or comfortable with her appearance until she dealt with her mother's distaste for all things feminine.

To truly understand our perception of ourselves, women have to consider the important role that their sexuality plays in the development of self-image. Comfort—or discomfort— with appearing sexy and feminine contributes to the way we perceive ourselves and then later affects our experience of changing looks. Feeling sexy for some women is equated with feeling beautiful. Menopause strikes these women differently than women for whom sexuality remains quietly in the background of their identities. As we undergo hormonal swings, women attribute different meanings to these changes. Some feel a great sense of loss, while others are glad to have sexuality become a nonissue.

Our mother's experience of sexuality is also important in understanding our self-image. Was she able to express her femininity? Or was she uncomfortable or even prudish, like Karen's mother seemed to be? It's not only our mother's experience of her own sexuality that impacts on our self-image, but our father's reaction to her that affects how we see ourselves as well. Surprisingly, sometimes our feminine role models are found in the generations that precede our parents.

Penny, a woman in her mid-50s shared the important role her grandparents' relationship had in soothing fears about getting older. Penny told us, *"What is most reassuring about looking older for me is watching my grandfather adore my grandmother. They're in their 90s and I often see them holding hands and rubbing each other's shoulders. My grandpa, to this day—he's 96—looks at Grannie with eyes that seem to say, 'You are the most beautiful, sexiest woman alive.' It can't be too bad to be 93 and still have someone feel that way about you."*

Penny had living proof that caring for her looks and feeling confident that a man could find her attractive as she aged, was not just an idea but a reality. As we listened to her story, it was unclear which came first, her grandmother's continued sense of beauty that stimulated her grandfather's interest, or his continued interest helping to perpetuate her grandmother's pleasure in her appearance. Our understanding is that this is most often a circular interpersonal experience. Regardless of the direction of these positive feelings, Penny's 93-year-old grandmother's beauty was clearly an encouraging story to hear.

Where does femininity fit in with your self-image? Was it an important element in your sense of attractiveness? Does your mother enjoy being a woman? Did she once feel that way, but doesn't now? These are keys to understanding the experience of our looks as we age; self-image is an amalgam of autobiographical perceptual memories that begins early in life, surfaces into consciousness during adolescence and ultimately congeals into a significant feature of our entire identity. All these experiences contribute to our self-image and are transmitted biologically and psychologically from one generation to the next—from grandmother to mother to daughter.

## Beauty Is in the "I" of the Beholder

Every woman in every generation grows up with idealized images of beauty. Maybe for Grandma, it was Carole Lombard, for Mom, it was Audrey Hepburn and for us, Jackie O. Our daughters' idols may range from Natalie Wood to Natalie Portman. Even as we age and our looks change, we maintain these images as standard definitions of beauty. Emma, a 59-year-old writer recalls, *"I wanted to have Sandra Dee's hair, Hayley Mills's smile, and Ann-Margret's body and those are still the images that come to my mind."* It is a challenge when we are surrounded by media that not-so-subtly implies the air-brushed, cover-girl beauty is the look of choice. Yet we need to remember that there is not just one quotient for beauty. Nothing could be more subjective. Your version may be a variation on a theme, a unique perception of what is deemed beautiful by society. That is the one that ultimately will matter most. This internal picture has more to do with the psychological reactions we have to our physical features—and the reactions others have had to us in the past—than any actual pictures can reveal.

. . .

**The development of our self-image involves a process that uniquely customizes the experience of beauty for every woman. Our self-image is neither static nor based on fixed physical features alone. It evolves over time and in the context of our surroundings.**

. . .

The question of perceived versus objective beauty is worth discussing a bit further. It raises an interesting paradox regarding the psychological eye of the beholder. Why do some women—like many of the models we work with—who are born with features that culture consensually validates as beautiful—so often report feeling unattractive? And how do women who, lacking these features, feel beautiful? Likewise, why do some women who develop fine lines around their eyes react with panic when they see these changes, while others with deeply etched crow's feet barely take notice? Once again, let's look at Mom's impact.

We return to Angeline, the former model whose internal dialogues were so self-critical. Although she appeared to be the vision of loveliness, she was not only fearful of aging out of a professional world, she had always felt like a fraud. We suspected that the seeds of this "deception" had taken root over the years of her young life, and Angeline validated this when she took us back in time.

Angeline lived for most of her life unable to enjoy her physical beauty. When we first met her in her 20s, she had already been featured on magazine covers and on fashion runways. By age 30, her career was fading. *"I started using drugs to get through photo shoots and then got addicted to cocaine. No one really stopped me, as long as they got the picture they wanted."* We were curious to find out if her family background could help explain Angeline's struggles. She said, *"No one in my family really knew what was going on. My mom never enjoyed my success . . . I think she was jealous of me. I've been told she was once attractive, but you'd never know that now. Her hair is bleached. She wears false eyelashes and pasty makeup. She looks awful. Oh, and she's always popping one pill or another. When I was growing up and lived at home, she and my dad used to argue about how I dressed, the makeup I wore, stuff like that. I developed early. Mom didn't like dad looking at me, especially when he told me I was pretty. How sad is that?"* At age 16, Angeline was 5' 11", thin, and noticed by a New York modeling scout. She left home and at 18, seemed to have it all, fame and fortune. By 20, Angeline was lost. *"I felt like a sham, fooling people into believing I was pretty. Drugs made that feeling easier to deal with."*

It's easy to see where Angeline's sense of fraudulence and insecurity came from. Whether a woman is visually appealing, but doesn't experience herself to be, or less attractive and does, lies in the makings of her self-image.

. . .

**The more we recognize that attractiveness is a subjective, developmental process which ultimately needs to satisfy the "I" of the beholder, the more we have the ability to take hold of that process and move forward.**

. . .

With some borrowed confidence in our belief that women can alter how we see ourselves, Angeline ultimately made fundamental changes to her self-image. She took Step Four and used her past experiences to help her move forward.

Angeline slowly began to understand why her confusing self-image and changing looks were so frightening to her. She realized she had never been able to identify with her mother—who had ambivalent feelings about her own beauty—and felt guilty enjoying her own attractiveness. Being looked at made her uncomfortable most of her life, stemming back to the mixed emotions she felt toward her father's admiration long ago. These early experiences left Angeline with a highly vulnerable self-image. With a great deal of internal work and years of changing the way she saw herself, Angeline said, *"Ironically, feeling beautiful came so late in my life. For the first time, after years of being unable to enjoy my appearance, I actually enjoy seeing myself as I really am."*

We ask other women to return to their experiences growing up, most particularly in relation to Mom, to understand the psychological underpinnings of the role appearance played in the development of their sense of self. We impress upon them that as unrelated as these old memories may seem, and as hard as it is to go backward, it is a key step to help them move forward. One way is to see the larger picture.

## Filling the Self-Image Reservoir

Sometimes we find the symbol of a reservoir useful in understanding the concept of self-image. This familiar image helps us visualize the fluid way physical and psychological factors blend to create our experience of beauty.

A typical reservoir is filled with provisions reserved for later use. A psychological reservoir is filled by life events and interactions that nourish our emotional lives. The quality of those experiences determines how we perceive ourselves (self-image) and how we feel about ourselves (self-esteem).

A reservoir filled with loving positive interactions nurtures our self-image and strengthens our self-esteem. Consequently, we can feel beautiful regardless of our objective physical appearance and maintain resilience in the face of criticism, rejection, and the changes we confront as we age. On the other hand, a reservoir filled with negativity, neglect, or criticism, does not nourish or support us, and a very different sense of self develops. While our lives may appear full, toxic relationships can leave us feeling empty; or even worse, they can erode our very foundation, resulting in poor self-image and low self-esteem. No matter how appealing our features or how highly we are regarded for them, we cannot retain pleasure derived from our appearance. Aging, unfortunately, often highlights this interpersonal phenomenon.

Recognizing self-image as an evolving and interactive developmental process is key to understanding and dealing with our looks as they change. It provides a perspective on beauty that is not static and gives support to the ability we all have to impact perception of ourselves as we age.

. . .

**As adults, our psychological reservoirs are ours to fill. Unlike the lack of choices we have growing up—such as our inability to select our own family and environment—we can gain control over many of those choices as we mature into adulthood. Instead of feeling a loss of control as we get older, we in fact have increased opportunities to fill our reservoir with responses that can now come from our own selves and from people we choose to have in our lives.**

. . .

Another way to comprehend the important role development has on our experience of our beauty is to see how assets other than appearance can be influenced by our familial and cultural environment. Understanding this will help you take emotional control over the changes you experience physically.

Alicia was deemed the beauty in her family. Her sister, Barbara, was a great athlete. Both were born with natural assets. Alicia had been encouraged to embellish her looks, and made to feel they would gain her success in life. Barbara showed early athletic skills and this was going to be the key to her success. As first-generation Asian immigrants, her parents wanted the best for both of them. Educated, pushed to achieve, Barbara was given every opportunity to become a serious athlete, Alicia to become popular and pretty.

Their dad, a short, stocky man, loved basketball and pushed Barbara hard with dreams that she become a professional athlete. No matter how well Barbara performed, her dad felt she could do better. He put a gym in their basement and a basketball hoop in the backyard. Barbara worked hard, but often felt she never was good enough. Although Barbara grew to be very skilled, she recalls never really enjoying her athleticism. Alicia told us, *"Poor Barbara. She put so much effort into being a good athlete, she missed having fun with her sport. By the time she was in college playing basketball, I think on some level she was relieved to get a break when she tore a hamstring during a game. She never really played well again and fell into a deep funk. She told me she felt there was nothing to make her worthwhile. She thought her life was over and I think it was because she could no longer please our dad. I couldn't convince her that it was really our parents' lives that were over, not hers. I had my issues about the pressure to look good, but they focused more on Barbara than me."*

It's easy to see how a child's experience of a physical asset can be influenced by how others respond to it, be it beauty or anything else, especially when it draws excessive attention. This also applies when too much focus is placed on a musical skill, mathematical mind, or any talent exhibited precociously in children. Ultimately, youthful beauty, like any asset, can fade with age, leaving in its place a deep sense of loss and emptiness needing to be filled as we become adults.

## WHAT FILLS YOUR RESERVOIR?

• • •

**The self-doubter:** Do you doubt yourself constantly? *("Please don't ask me to give that speech . . . I'll look awful, I'll make a mess of it.")* It's possible that your reservoir has previously been filled by criticism. You may have heard others doubt you and then, as often happens, you begin to believe those voices. Try talking back to the critic, and fill your reservoir with the confidence you are gaining as you read this book.

**The neglected:** Do you fail to care for yourself? Avoid trying to improve your appearance? *("What's the difference at this point?")* Your reservoir feels empty. You may have been neglected, emotionally and physically, and have internalized the neglect that previously surrounded you. You may treat yourself now the way you were once treated. Just because you lived with others who didn't put much stock in caring for you or your "beauty," doesn't mean you need to neglect yourself. Fill yourself up with attention and care.

**The competitor:** Do you compare yourself to others? Compete with much younger women? *("I'll show them who looks better in jeans!")* You may have been compared to others growing up, to your siblings or friends, but isn't it time to fill that reservoir with a little well-earned maturity? In sports they call it going for your "personal best." Do the same with your own unique self.

**The perfectionist:** Do you constantly fall short of a standard you set for yourself, or if you reach your goals, always feel you can do more? *("The chemical peel worked, why not go for something bigger?")* Your reservoir was likely filled by expectations that you be perfect, or at least better than you are. The media feeds that perception as well. Fill your reservoir with reasonable expectations.

**The guilty:** Do you blame yourself for almost everything, including aging? *("Honey, I've tried everything, but nothing I do makes me look like I used to.")* Your reservoir may have been filled with self-admonishments and apologies. You may feel undeserving, which makes it hard to feel good about *looking* good. Try filling your reservoir with more forgiveness and acceptance.

If we approach our appearance from this developmental perspective, it is easier to understand and become more forgiving of our mothers. Remember, it's very likely that they filled our reservoirs much the way theirs were filled by their parents. History tends to repeat itself unless we become cognizant of our own psychological processes. With awareness, we have the possibility of altering the course of how we see ourselves and ultimately how our children view us.

By taking control over the voices that once controlled us, we can shift our current sense of attractiveness and potentially reconfigure the definition of beauty as we age. With this perspective, we can also recognize the impact we have on our daughters' experience of themselves—how they see themselves now and as they age. If we focus less on one narrow standard of beauty, we have an opportunity and power to help the next generation respond more receptively to our changing looks, seeing them through a different lens. We can use our deeper and broader understanding of "beauty" to move forward both as daughters and as parents.

## Our Mothers, Ourselves

For many of us, our mothers' generation had little inherent power except their looks. A wrinkle for them could quickly rise to the catastrophic. For some, powerlessness led to apathy, desperation, letting looks go, and reaching "old age" at a time when many of us are going strong. While our generation has far more power to shape our journey through life, the maternal role models we grew up watching may remain our templates of aging.

Ariel told us she didn't know anyone else whose mom had a face-lift as hers did in her 60s. *"I had no idea what to make of it. My mom had always been gorgeous to me, but I realize looking back that she was obsessed with her appearance. It's too bad, because she had it all . . . natural, thick, black hair, big blue eyes, and a great body. But she didn't take to getting older well. She seemed panicked as her looks changed. My dad thought she was crazy when she decided to get her first face-lift. It was kept a secret from me. All I knew was that she went away for a couple of weeks to my grandma's in Florida. I barely noticed the change. It looked like she went on vacation. When she had her third one, I barely recognized her. I came home*

*from college and I'll never forget how scary she looked . . .
bright red lipstick and blue eye shadow and not the mom I
knew. I was almost scared to hug her. It was as if her face
looked frozen in fear. Ugh. That'll never happen to me."*

Ah, but it can, unless we choose to become more aware and
make different choices. Unfortunately, it is not often clear how
to recognize alternatives. Even though our mothers lived in
different times, their fear of aging is absorbed and transmitted
to us, so that we tend to repeat their experience, feel their
fears, and react the way they reacted. The less aware we are of
this process, the more automatically and similarly we seem to
respond. There are those who wish their mothers had shared
more of their feelings: *"If nothing else, I wish she would have told
me to enjoy my looks while I was young,"* says one woman, 59,
echoing how many feel. She has nothing specifically negative
to say about how her mother raised her but realizes she can be
more open and honest with her two teenage daughters.

But even those daughters, and other well-nurtured girls
who grow up with a balanced sense of beauty, are challenged
by the complicated messages that come from outside the home.
When we met Beth, she had just come from the unsettling
experience she had at her husband's studio. She was still trying
to figure out this brain vs. beauty dilemma, though as an adult
she was quick to understand where it came from.

Beth recalled that her physical appearance didn't
matter to her that much growing up. As far back as
she remembered, she wanted to do well in school
and become a teacher like her mom. We were curious about Beth's family. *"I wasn't especially pretty
when I was little, but I always felt my parents thought
I was. I knew other girls were more attractive, but my
parents made me feel confident about my looks. My problem was trying to be smart and popular. Sounds like a
lucky problem to have, but being part of the 'in' group in
high school meant not caring about grades, which didn't*

*work for me."* Beth said she remembers deciding to keep her academic interests quiet, except at home. *"I felt proud of my good grades, but hid them from my friends. And I kept my interests in clothes and makeup out of my house. My parents thought they were silly. The two just didn't mix."*

Now, as a college professor at 52, Beth was stymied by the confusion she felt, a kind of self-doubt she hadn't experienced since she was an adolescent. *"I've been very busy with teaching and my family for so many years, but recently I've had some regrets that I didn't pay more attention to my appearance. I've become more aware how other women my age seem younger and dress more fashionably and I don't like the feeling that I look old. I am happy my parents didn't emphasize superficial things. But I feel torn, like I did back then, between paying attention to my looks and staying true to the other values that matter to me. At least now I don't have to hide that I'm smart. It's exposing that I care about my looks; that is hard for me."*

Beth's maturity and openness helped her resolve these paradoxical pulls, ultimately finding a more comfortable way to manage them. How we handle our changing looks and the degree to which we experience these changes as acceptable, painful, or devastating has a lot to do with how our mothers negotiated their aging process. We might not like to recognize their influence, but in spite of our determination to be different or better, we not only recapitulate their experience, but perhaps attempt to rewrite the end of the script.

Remember Julie, who was desperate to have a fourth child? We asked about her history to understand why bearing more children might serve to mask her fears about aging. She told us that she associated pregnancy not only with the happiest times in her own life, but also in her mother's. This was mostly a fantasy, a way Julia wanted to remember her mom, since in reality her mother had become quite depressed after having children. In fact, she reminded herself that after her mom had her last child, she never seemed the same. She was depressed, seemed to slow down, was less fun loving, and aged quickly. *"My mom had four kids, was totally overwhelmed and my dad was of little help. He worked long hours . . . we all thought he had another love interest. In some ways we didn't blame him. Mom was so devoted to us, maybe too much so. She didn't pay much attention to herself. She let her hair go gray. Barely wore makeup. Dad was very critical of her looks. I think that's what really scares me. She gave up. I'm not ready for that."*

Julie's yearning to have more children appeared rooted in her desire to feel empowered. Using this insight, Julie considered that it wasn't another child she needed, but rather an understanding of her history that could allow her to make better choices than her mother had.

Finally, there are those women who contend that their mothers have nothing to do with how they feel about aging. They plan to manage their changing looks differently. Those are strong, healthy, optimistic sentiments, but they aren't always easy to put into action.

Take Alana, our model who was panicking about life after modeling. When she was growing up, she said, *"I couldn't see myself in my mom. She was from a different generation and a different world. She was born in Russia and she didn't focus on her looks. Her life was about making a better life for her kids. My mom cleaned homes and my dad was a plumber. That was it, hard work. My life was so different. A talent scout discovered me when I was 15, and the rest is history. I bought a house for my parents, who live comfortably now. They're retired and don't do much. They're old . . . actually, they're in their 60s, but my mom looks like she could be my grandma. That's not what my life is about and never will be. I plan to stay looking good for the rest of my life. I'll never look like her."*

Doth she protest too much? Is Alana in denial, or, in fact, does the next generation have it better? At times, we may even feel a bit guilty at having more opportunities than our mothers to live longer, more vital lives, and as a result, feel unable to enjoy the advantages. Or, sometimes it's how our fathers dealt with our mothers' aging processes that affects us.

Remember Hannah, who was finding it hard to keep her spirits up, and became down on herself as she looked in the mirror at the gym? Her internal dialogues led her to memories of her father who dramatically aged after his bike accident. Going further into the details of her history, she recalled, *"It wasn't just that my dad's life changed. It was my mom, too. They were in their 50s when it happened and his anger spilled over into everything. He used to be affectionate with my mom. They loved to dance in our living room to old show tunes. Once he had to use a cane he started withdrawing. I think he gave up on his life, and my mom gave up, too. She seemed to take his cue that both their lives were over and never cared for herself after that. For her, looking good was over by age 50."*

As in therapy, we want you to use an understanding of your personal history to make sense of feelings now. Examine your relationship to your mother, your father and your parents' relationship to each other. Look carefully at possible roots of your self-image. Take into account that human nature leads us to repeat history unless we take active measures to change the patterns we learn and absorb. If you know from where you came, changing the course of your future is possible. Insight requires awareness. Change requires effort. Who knows? If you can liberate yourself from your past, you may even find more compassion for your less liberated mom, and take her off that psychological hot seat once and for all.

Now we move on to explore the stage in women's development when the consolidation of self-image is most challenged. It will help you understand similar challenges your face now as an adult, when your self-image is again confronted by fundamental changes. Adolescence, here we come again.

## Using Your Family History to Clarify Your Feelings about Changing Looks

► Recall how your parents saw you as a young girl. What words were used when you were introduced to others? For example, were you called the cutie pie, princess, fatty, smarty pants?

► Did your looks play a small or large role in your relationship to your family?

► Were there any other significant people in your childhood that may have had a role in how you saw yourself?

► Describe your mother's appearance when she was a young woman (either from memory or photographs). If she is still living, how does she look now? How would you describe your mother's sense of femininity?

► Did you want to be like her? Do you want to be like her now?

► Do you recall a time you saw yourself as pretty? As unattractive? Do you have a memory when someone else saw you as pretty?

► Take a look at pictures of yourself when you were a child, an adolescent. Hold them side by side to pictures of yourself now. Note your reaction.

► Take a look at pictures of your mom when she was your age now. Think about how you feel looking at these pictures.

# chapter seven

• • •

## Adolescence in Residence

*I feel like I have become the person I wanted
to be when I was 15 or 16.*

— Kristin Scott Thomas

### Step Five: Looking Back to Move Forward

You've been there before and it's probably the last place you want to revisit. Call it "Adolescence: The Sequel." Sure, you're dealing with sunspots instead of pimples, drooping breasts rather than developing ones. But let's face it: girls and midlife women are often having the same conversations. Do either of these sound familiar?

Two teenage girls were talking over lunch about their summer plans. One was going to India to take a course in comparative religion. The other was headed to Africa on an environmental study program. Both were absorbed in the exchange of ideas about spiritualism and global warming. As they parted, one said, *"I hear there's this really cute guy on my trip."* The other asked, *"Are you taking your UGGs?"*

Two women in their 40s were debating presidential politics. Teachers at the same high school, they disagreed about the candidates' health policies. But they did agree to meet later for a consultation at Brite Smile, and maybe drop into Bloomies to pick up a new anti-aging cream. They left debating the benefits of Retinol over exfoliants.

How do girls and women veer from being engaged in intellectual pursuits to such trivial matters? How can we shift so seamlessly from selflessness to self-absorption? They didn't teach us this in study hall but it is Step Five: mastering adolescence at midlife.

## Is Fifty the New Fifteen?

Our fears and concerns about how we look—as well as the measures to allay those fears—are remarkably similar during these key transitional stages. Granted, it may not be groundbreaking news that at 50, many of us feel like we're 15 again. Yet you'd be surprised how many women are ashamed and keeping it secret from one another. Our preoccupation with appearance isn't accidental. Both of these "beauty bookends" are besieged with mixed cultural messages: young girls are encouraged to study hard, try out for sports, run for office . . . but don't forget the hair and makeup. By contrast, midlifers are allegedly admired for their wisdom but at the same time told *not look their age!*

The results? A generation of Miley Cyrus and Britney Spears wannabes trying to speed up the clock and a generation of otherwise smart women trying to slow theirs down. Together we are stuck in what we have coined the beauty paradox, the web of conflicting forces pulling us in opposite directions regarding our feelings about our looks.

• • •

**Step Five is about focusing on the significant similarities— and disparities—between these two phases of development.**

**There are parallels that are both physical and psychological, the latter being harder to identify since they are less tangible and visible.**

. . .

Let's face it: In adolescence, we are letting go of our youth and fearful of growing up. In midlife, we are letting go of the last *vestiges* of youth and fearful of growing old. In both, we sometimes find ourselves holding on too long, for fear of moving on. Yet the more we hold on, the less comfortable we feel in our new skins.

| PHYSICAL PARALLELS | |
| --- | --- |
| **ADOLESCENCE:**<br>**What Goes Up** | **MIDLIFE:**<br>**Must Come Down** |
| a) onset of menses | a) menopause |
| b) increasing hormones | b) decreasing hormones |
| c) increased sex drive | c) decreased libido |
| d) skin breakouts | d) skin sags, wrinkles |
| e) hair growth | e) hair grays, thins |
| f) rounding bodies | f) softening muscles, metabolism slows |
| g) bone growth | g) brittle bones, decreasing height |
| h) preoccupation with physical self | h) preoccupation with physical self |

For starters, try to think back on how you dealt with some of the physical transitions in your adolescence. You'll find that your memories of these changes likely resonate with midlife realities. Breaking out was hard to do? Well, wrinkles are even harder to deal with, as they make their grand entrance and never leave. Competition at 50, over whose face-lift looks better or whose neck is tighter, harkens back to competition over which girls had hotter bodies and wore cooler clothes. Author Rachel Simmons recalls, *"Ask any 50-year-old woman if she remembers who was the most popular girl in her eighth-grade class and she'll know."*

Both then and now, transitions can be fraught with conflict as we are pulled in different directions.

As a preteen, Leslie overcame initial self-consciousness and worked hard to create a look. *"I made sure I dressed in the latest styles and spent a lot of time trying to appear as if I didn't care."* Inwardly, her appearance was vitally important. Over time it all became second nature. Throughout the following decades, meticulous about her clothes and makeup, she pulled off looking great quite easily. Recently, she found that it took much more time trying to hide her imperfections—the visible lines around her mouth, the bulge she couldn't keep off her middle. Jewelry, scarves, and accessories had always added to her look. Now they drew attention to places she didn't want it drawn. The day of her surprise 50th birthday party she had a full-blown panic attack. *"My heart raced, I was sweating buckets. I ran to the bathroom to try to calm down and kept thinking as I looked in the mirror that I wish I had spent more time fixing myself that morning. I can't believe what is happening to me!"* She remembered she hadn't been sleeping well lately, waking up several times a night from hot flashes, her sheets wet with sweat.

*"I wonder if there are sweat spots on my silk shirt? How disgusting!"* She imagined everyone would be thinking, *"How un–Leslie like."* The people she worked with seemed younger and younger and she worried

she might lose her job to some kid out of college. *"How could that happen when I feel I'm better at my job than ever before?"* She felt her experience showed on her aging face and that she didn't fit in anymore. *"I'm just out of sorts, moody, irritable . . . I haven't felt this insecure since I was a young girl."* When would this end? And where did the end lead? And why did it matter so much?

Leslie later admitted that as a youngster she had been extremely shy about her changing body, even among her peers. She was the girl hiding in the stalls until everyone else had gone, before changing into her swimsuit. Now, all these years later she was, once again, suffering alone. Yet the truth is, had Leslie asked almost anyone if her job was in jeopardy, she would likely have gotten the reassurance she needed. She was still that chic, smart woman others admired. For Leslie, adolescence had taken up residence at age 50, throwing wisdom and maturity into rewind.

## Why Then Matters Now

At age 50, Leslie may have been too caught up in her current anxieties to use her past to help her with her present. These transitional times, in adolescence and at midlife, serve important functions in our development and if we use that perspective we have a lot to gain. Remember, you have been there before. Teen turbulence does pass, so too will this phase.

Even for women whose identities are less attached to appearance, facing an aging face can be distressing. Whether we thought of ourselves as attractive or not, we may have grown up relying on other qualities for our sense of security in other ways. Today, we may be the most surprised by our strong reactions to what we see in the mirror.

Certain her husband, a successful jazz musician, was losing interest in her, Linda constantly worried that he might be having an affair while on tour, even though he denied this vehemently. There were days she called him ten times, just to find out where he was, who he was with, and whether he was thinking about her. *"It's so weird, I haven't done that since high school, when I worried about whether I was still someone's best friend, or if I was being excluded from whatever was going on over a weekend. I used to drive my friends nuts."*

She wasn't as focused on her looks back then—it was more about being connected to a crowd. *"I never thought much about how I looked because I never was that attractive,"* she confessed. *"That's not what I built my self-esteem on. I was the fun one, made people laugh, even made fun of myself to make people laugh. That's what my husband loved about me. But I find myself looking in the mirror these days and I'm seeing changes that make me feel that same kind of feeling I had back in my teens. It's insecurity about my place in my life, about who really cares about me and why."* Linda said she felt invisible, even though physically she felt far from invisible. She was heavier than she had ever been. *"I've gained so much weight. I can't even look at myself. I haven't felt this lack of confidence in so long. I hate it."*

Looking into her rearview mirror, we recognized that Linda tried to get attention as an adolescent in order to feel that people were connecting to her. Now, this same need for acknowledgment resurfaced in her marriage. Even though her husband tried to reassure Linda that she was as attractive to him as the day they met, the words fell on deaf ears. She felt irrationally focused on how she was losing control over her husband, her body, and her life, so much so that her work and her children were being neglected.

Linda was attaching old emotions to her new situation. Had she connected her present feelings to her adolescent ones, and talked about them with her husband, she might have avoided long periods of discord. The energy she directed toward getting to the bottom of her husband's "alleged" disloyalty would have been better directed toward dealing with her own anxieties. While it seems that her appearance now is the issue for Linda, what was really going on was the reliving of adolescent fears about not being noticed.

For many women, rewinding is necessary and helpful. Can you recall how you handled transitions in the past? Did you have trouble being dropped off at school? Years later, did you beg to have your room left exactly as it was, even after you left home for college? All are rather common responses to changes as children, and they seem mild now compared to awakening hormones and the creeping cleavage of adolescence, or the declining hormones and drooping cleavage of midlife.

An attractive nurse today, at 57, Marie still vividly recalls the day she got her first period. *"I was sitting in my Spanish class and suddenly felt something wet underneath. When I looked down, I saw this dark red color. I was mortified. I didn't know any other girls who'd started. I ran out of class to the lavatory, threw my underwear into the trash and then went to the nurse's office and said I was sick. I was sort of a tomboy so I felt confused and even mad that I was into this feminine thing. My mom kept telling me I was a woman now, trying to make me feel better. I couldn't stop crying. Now I'm premenopausal and I can't stop crying again."*

This time, of course it was because the flow had stopped. In adolescence, the body a girl knows is no longer there. From a time of emotional ease, she is thrust into upheaval, with fluctuating hormones, unpredictable mood swings, and sexual sensations. Such a state of affairs is recapitulated during menopause.

· · ·

**In adolescence, you may become unrecognizable to your parents but in menopause, more alarmingly, you become unrecognizable to yourself!**

· · ·

| PSYCHOLOGICAL PARALLELS | |
|---|---|
| **ADOLESCENCE:**<br>**What Begins Here** | **MIDLIFE:**<br>**Must End Here** |
| a) Separation from family, greater connection to peers | a) Separation from aging parents, children leaving home, greater need for friends |
| b) Clinging to childhood, moving on to adulthood | b) Clinging to youth, moving through midlife and beyond |
| c) Moodiness, out-of-control feelings, especially anxiety and loss | c) Moodiness, out-of-control feelings, especially anxiety and loss |
| d) Identity consolidation—attaching aspects of self to self-image, creating template for adulthood | d) Identity reconstruction—detaching aspects of self associated with youth, including beauty and fertility—to create a new sense of self |

## Too Late for Temper Tantrums

Aspects of identity and self-image become cohesive during adolescence. Our identities become strongly wrapped around all that we internalized up until then and continue on course much that same way throughout adulthood. In midlife this cohesion undergoes an upheaval, having to unravel in order to be re-created.

As this happens, most women feel disoriented, as if the basis of their feminine identity is destabilized. Are you coping now as you did or didn't in adolescence during these changing times? Take a look at the table on page 107 that shows the parallels between common adolexcent and midlife behaviors.

Acting out, rebelling, and sexual experimentation during adolescence are natural developmental reactions to change. We mostly write these behaviors off to "those terrible teen years." But how does that translate at midlife? We're definitely too old for temper tantrums and an affair might be appealing if our estrogen levels still had a pulse. But neither will ultimately resolve our current changes. That being said, for many women we talk to, the coping tactics at midlife are far too similar to those they used as young girls.

A petite, athletic tennis instructor, Justine was once a Division One college player. She was most at home on the tennis court, but recently found herself pulled away to spend time caring for her ailing 77-year-old diabetic mother. Over the past year, Justine had lost about 15 pounds. She realized that anxiety was contributing to losing weight, but she couldn't stop herself from slipping into compulsive exercise patterns. Envied by many of her peers who kept putting on weight at this age, Justine knew she was headed to a self-destructive place reminiscent of her teens.

An eating disorder had plagued her for years. She fainted on a tennis court at 16, which propelled her to get help. Among the things she had learned was how she controlled the intake of food to manage fears about her changing body, sexuality, and becoming an adult. For many years after, her weight and her sense of how she looked stabilized. Although looking and feeling fit mattered to her throughout college and her career, she maintained a balance between her health and her looks.

Until now. *"It was a double whammy when my dad died and my mom's diabetes got worse,"* Justine explained. *"That's when I started having these issues again."* It was about the same time she decided to go back to competing and began training for the Nationals, a challenging 40-and-older tennis event. Being out of the tournament circuit for a while, this one required enormous preparation and helped distract her from some of the other events in her life. *"I haven't felt this out of control in years,"* Justine said.

Events in Justine's current life triggered a shift in her identity reminiscent of changes in adolescence. Her reaction was to resort to old coping measures, like dieting and excessive exercising, behaviors she had previously used to deal with anxiety. Justine needed to recognize her feelings so she could face the real issues that needed to be resolved. She had to mourn her father and face the sadness she felt about her ailing mother. Only then could she move toward filling these empty spaces with her own more hopeful future. She had to allow the changes in her body and life to find a new home, not by stopping a natural process of transition, but by taking control of her feelings through understanding.

In a certain way, Justine was fortunate. At least she was aware that she was reacting in midlife much as she had in adolescence. It provided helpful insight toward breaking a vicious pattern, which is the beginning of almost any change of behavior. Other women either aren't conscious of the revival of old feelings, work hard to *avoid* remembering them, or even displace them onto others.

| DEFIANCE AND DENIAL IN ADOLESCENCE AND MIDLIFE | |
|---|---|
| **ADOLESCENCE:** Fight and Defy | **MIDLIFE:** Fight and Defy |
| a) Aggressive and rebellious behavior | a) Aggressive and rebellious behavior |
| b) Promiscuity, sexual experimentation | b) Promiscuity, leaving role as wife and parent, having affairs |
| c) Inappropriate behavior, acting like someone older, dressing as an adult | c) Inappropriate behavior, acting like someone younger, dressing like a teenager |
| d) Impulsive behavior, addictions, food issues | d) Impulsive behavior, addictions, compulsive shopping |
| **ADOLESCENCE:** Fight and Deny | **MIDLIFE:** Fight and Deny |
| a) Avoidance behavior, self-neglect | a) Avoidance behavior, self-neglect |
| b) Numbing self through drugs, alcohol, sleep | b) Numbing self through drugs, alcohol, sleep |
| c) Clinging to childlike behavior patterns and parents | c) Clinging to old behavior patterns, like over-protective parenting |
| d) Isolation and withdrawal | d) Isolation and withdrawal |

A 51-year-old divorced single mom, Patricia originally sought help to understand the trouble she was having with Emily, her 17-year-old daughter. She had a list of concerns: Emily wore too much makeup, dressed inappropriately, and hung out with a reckless group of friends. Patricia was convinced that these behaviors were Emily's way of dealing with low self-esteem and wondered if it might be related to her daughter's bad skin. *"Acne runs in our family and I don't want her to do what I did when I was a teenager. I used to try to act cool to compensate for how awkward I felt. I became promiscuous, got into trouble. I tried to do anything to be part of the 'in' crowd."*

Although it was clear that Patricia didn't endorse Emily's behavior, it appeared that her preoccupation with her daughter's "beauty" issues was in part distracting her from her own. With a bit of prompting, Patricia revealed that her own adolescent experiences with acne had left her with permanent scarring, both emotional and physical. Patricia remembered getting little help from her own parents, who were uncomfortable about her teenage struggles and ignored them. Emily, on the other hand, didn't think she had any serious problems and was annoyed by her mother's constant offerings of solutions, including therapists and acne creams. Patricia almost seemed envious that her daughter could get through this difficult period more easily than she had and was unable to see that her daughter's experience could be different than her own.

Patricia was a devoted parent, but her over-identification with Emily's problems was straining their relationship and interfering with Patricia's ability to care for herself. She admitted that when she caught a glance of herself in the pharmacy mirror, it brought her right back to her own adolescent angst. *"That can't be me!"* she thought. The lines creasing her forehead and the folds of skin sagging around her neck horrified her. She felt anxious and upset by the feelings she thought she had left behind years ago when she had once been so preoccupied by her face. Occasionally, she thought about trying one of the many age-defying creams that filled the shelf next to the acne-defying ones, but dealing with her daughter's changing appearance seemed easier than focusing on her own. Clearly it was not too late for Patricia to care for herself, but she needed to be guided in the right direction.

We can unintentionally do the wrong things for the right reasons. Patricia's concern about her daughter's behavior clearly was motivated by feelings of love and protection. Rather than remembering and focusing on her own adolescence, Patricia was reliving it through her daughter and trying to provide interventions and solutions that she herself might have wanted. In the end, however, her behavior only alienated Emily from her. The paradoxical feelings in adolescence—hold on, but move on—were striking both females of the family but only one was looking forward.

## Looking Toward an "Empty Next"

Granted, the future for midlife women doesn't immediately seem rosy. While girls like Emily are moving into exciting new possibilities, women like Patricia are facing decreasing choices. Teenage girls are challenged by figuring out the role beauty will play in their lives, leaving behind childlike dependency, moving toward increased independence. Midlife women often move reluctantly from caring for children—and more ambivalently, from tending their aging parents—while physical attributes are clearly *exiting* the equation.

It doesn't have to be viewed as the "empty next." Let's think half full and use our previous transitional experiences to teach us to manage this one better. So, for example, did you take your looks for granted growing up and then in midlife convince yourself your appearance didn't matter? Did you resent the importance beauty had in your life and still do now?

Susan, manager of her own successful P.R. firm, recalls, *"As smart as I was, both as a young student and in my career, I know that my looks helped get me a lot of work. And I can't deny that I played it up in how I dressed and flirted. My mom taught me well. She was one of my greatest fans, loved to take me shopping and spent gobs of money my dad said we didn't have."* At one point in her career, Susan was referred to not just as a blonde but as a "blonde bombshell." Today, in her late 50s, Susan is seriously overweight and does not doubt that, *"as I got older, it almost became easier to just let it all go. Maybe the last thing I wanted to be described as was a former blond bombshell. Being fat was somehow easier."*

Susan was the young girl many of us aspired to be: a stellar student with herds of males circling at all times. As a young adult, she began to wonder how much of her success was based on brains, how much on beauty. In midlife, she neglected her appearance. She didn't let herself enjoy her looks, gaining enough weight to be considered obese. Susan claims to be enjoying a new kind of "liberation," but her friends feel she's gone too far and frankly, worry about her health. We understood this as an expression of revived ambivalence she felt over the role her beauty played in her life.

Ambivalence dies hard, as does envy. Heather, a top student in high school, went on to Stanford and is now a prestigious lawyer and commentator teaching law at Georgetown. Yet she revealed that at her recent high school reunion, she went nervously up to Abigail, former homecoming queen, now stay-at-home mother of five, and said, *"I still remember the purple and yellow dress you wore the first day of tenth grade."*

At a party on New York's Upper East Side, Megan, one of the city's most glamorous women, entered and began greeting her friends. Now in her early 50s, she was sporting a pouty new set of lips and an oddly frozen forehead. One of the guests, Lindsey, a successful but rather modest-looking writer, whispered to another, *"Why wasn't I born with her genes?"* Her friend responded, *"She's clearly having a harder time aging than we are!"*

Let's face it: regardless of how successful we are, when it comes to insecurity over changing looks, we fall into old—as in young!—patterns. And just as we envied those beautiful girls in our teens, so do we envy them now at midlife. The truth is, no one, not even the prettiest girl you recall from high school, is exempt from the loss and the changes that come with age. We know from our experience working with young models that they don't escape these fears, living with anticipation of the new faces that will replace them. It's a practiced art to appear beautiful, while looking carefree and natural. These beautiful and envied women, far from relaxed in their good looks, experience an intensified version of what many women feel as we hit midlife.

## They Like Me, Do They Really Like Me?

It may seem difficult to imagine, but many of the models and celebrities we meet claim to have been—or at least felt like—unattractive, awkward adolescents. Cover girl Gisele Bündchen recalls, *"The kids in school called me Olive Oyl. I was taller than every guy in my class. Especially at that age, you think you're the weirdest thing that ever walked on earth."* Only much later do these women realize that they often use their careers as a means to obtain from the outside what they didn't feel on the inside. A natural reaction may be to feel little sympathy for their plight, but who knows what it really feels like to be Michelle Pfeiffer or Uma Thurman at 15 or 50? The gorgeous Joan Crawford seemed comfortable with the attention her beauty brought her for most of her adult life, until she turned 60. At that time, the story goes that she was shown a few unflattering photos and basically went into isolation until the day she died. It would be interesting to know how she fared her changing looks at adolescence and see if there were parallels that would help understand her midlife difficulties.

Even public figures who seem to fare better through their changing looks struggle to get there. Sally Field, for example, has spoken about feeling unsure of herself as an adolescent, using acting skills to compensate for her lack of confidence and other teenage insecurities. Her roles as Gidget and the Flying Nun were less about her beauty and more about her spunky personality. But even she faced barren times as she entered her 40s and 50s. Like many female actors, Field could no longer rely on her youthful persona to secure work. Fortunately, she put vanity aside and found great character roles that allowed her to "act her age"—as Forrest Gump's mother and most recently, as the complex matriarch in the TV series *Brothers and Sisters.*

Yet no one will forget Field's famous speech at the 1985 Oscars when she openly exposed her need for reassurance and acceptance. Like an insecure adolescent, she gushed, *"I've wanted more than anything to have your respect . . . this time I feel it, and I can't deny the fact that you like me, right now, you like me."* Now at 62, the actress seems to feel the self-confidence that eluded her. She serves as spokeswoman for products promoting healthy choices for midlife women and has become a model for aging well.

For everyday women, models and celebrities alike, we emphasize the importance in understanding adolescence as a tool toward resolving our complex feelings about changing looks. Rather than deny or dread this new period of change— so parallel to the one we experienced years ago—we encourage recognition of the commonalities, use hindsight for insight, and take time to gain perspective about how we dealt with adolescent changes, and how our family dealt with us during those times. It will help in not only becoming better, wiser parents to our children, but to ourselves as well. Understanding the pulls within and around us at that time is critical in moving forward at this one.

## Using Adolescent Experiences to Help Manage the Present

- How did you deal with the changes in your body in your teens?

- How did you deal with changes in your relationships with family and friends?

- Are there similarities between both phases?

- Did the media exert a strong influence on your choices as a teen? Does it now?

- Although you may want to rewind the clock, try fast-forwarding instead. Imagine yourself 20 years in the future, looking at pictures of yourself now. Think how you will feel about how you look. You will probably think you look great and might regret that you didn't enjoy your midlife beauty when you had the opportunity.

- If adolescence was a blur, don't let midlife be one, too. Use your teenage memories in combination with your adult perspective to help you make better choices now.

# chapter eight

. . .

## Say Good-bye to Say Hello

*People are like stained-glass windows.*
*They sparkle and shine when the sun is out, but*
*when the darkness sets in, their true beauty is*
*revealed only if there is a light from within.*

— Elisabeth Kübler-Ross

### Step Six: Moving Forward

All women report feeling some sense of loss when their appearance changes: loss of beauty, loss of youth, loss of control. Perhaps all three. Our next and final step is about letting go, making a shift and creating room for healthier emotional alternatives to our changing looks. This step requires us to experience losses that are unique to this phase of life, arousing feelings that often surprise women with their intensity and pervasiveness into otherwise stable lives.

We learned in previous chapters that the reactions to loss are quite variable depending upon the role looks play in our identity, our personal history, and the sturdiness of our sense of self. Accepting emotional change as a result of loss is called the process of mourning. Even if we don't see it staring us in the face, mourning is as inevitable as aging itself.

. . .

The key to Step Six is to learn how to let go of old definitions of beauty and make room for expanded ones. This
step requires learning to include our appearance as only one
among many other assets that define who we are. Identities
with a broader base provide women more stability and flexibility even as looks change.

. . .

We are entering a phase of life when, rather than caving in,
women can keep growing and become even more authentically
and beautifully ourselves. For our generation—which has reached
par on so many levels—it is a challenge worth meeting.

Think of Step Six as turning loss into potential gain.

## The Way We Were

Aging, at all phases of life, means leaving behind one
stage to move on to another. Consequently, every stage has
a beginning and an end, and involves letting go, sometimes
with sadness—*"she's not a baby anymore"* or *"those were the
good ole days"*—sometimes with relief—*"good riddance to those
terrible twos and terrifying teens."* In our last chapter, we saw
how adolescence is about bidding adieu to aspects of youth as
we move toward adulthood. Not without turbulence and not
without the help of parents and peers, this move requires the
leaving behind of dependency to attain increased freedom and
responsibility.

As we separate from our families and enter adulthood, our
physical, perceptual, and emotional experience of ourselves
takes shape and becomes firmly rooted into our identities.
Although many of us go through major events in the years that
follow—including marriage, motherhood, career development,
and divorce, to name a few—this visual image of ourselves

remains relatively stable for much of adulthood. The way we were settles into the way we are for a long middle act.

And we seem most content there. The emotions we attach to the development of self-image were explored in a survey we distributed to women between the ages 25–65 (see Appendix A). One of the questions asked was, "If you had to choose an age that most closely represents a picture of how you see yourself, when would that be?" Interestingly, a large majority said that while they may wish they were still in their early 20s, their mid-30s was the time when their perception of themselves seemed to freeze. When asked why, one response summarized many others, *"Since turning 30, I settled into a look that basically has stayed with me until now."*

Perhaps as hormonal fluctuations calm down after adolescence, or perhaps as we become distracted by other life challenges—jobs, relationships, and new families—we have less interest and time to focus on our appearance. It's as if an image forms and becomes relatively fixed.

Like Professor Henry Higgins, who wistfully sang about the *"face"* he had *"grown accustomed to,"* we too become attached to the most familiar and comfortable image we have of ourselves.

## First, the Bad News: Mourning an Unexpected Loss

Given that the process of letting go and moving on is part of the natural evolution of life, you'd think this process would be pretty well rehearsed by now. But are we really ready for this next close-up? There has to be an explanation why otherwise smart, evolved women are acting so foolishly, getting stuck as they cling desperately to old versions of themselves, physically and emotionally warding off natural life changes.

We believe the answer lies in the fact that women are unaware of, or unable to tolerate, the particular kind of mourning process required at this phase of life. It is different from other kinds of mourning and in certain ways more difficult, because the loss often remains intangible and inaccessible.

● ● ●

**Comfort with our changing appearance requires mourning an aspect of ourselves deeply embedded in our identities. Unfortunately our culture conspires to keep this awareness hidden from us.**

● ● ●

Like a pebble tossed into a pond, changing looks at this stage of life leads to a ripple effect that is ever expanding and increasingly confusing, hitting us in the farthest reaches of our identities. Not only do we anticipate losing our youth, but these changes awaken losses reminiscent of ones in our past. They stimulate not only sadness, but feelings of rejection, disappointment, and anger as we anticipate detaching from identities we had as vital and appealing women. It's no wonder we move gingerly toward futures as marginalized women. No wonder we hold on to avoid loss.

## Attaching and Detaching

It is commonly believed that women experience attachment and loss differently than men. We may vie for equality in other ways, but when it comes to the expression of emotions, we're just not the same as men. We still tend to cry more often, whether it be watching Leonardo DiCaprio and Kate Winslet sinking at sea in *Titanic*, fathers giving their daughters away, or parents being buried. We tend to have a harder time leaving our children on their first day of kindergarten, or years later when they move into college dorms. Women just seem to allow themselves—or are hardwired that way—to be more attached. Therefore, we are vulnerable when we emotionally detach.

So it is, when we let go of the image of ourselves that we have been attached to all throughout adulthood. Remember, our self-image has remained relatively stable, with little change following our adolescence. It is the self-portrait we've taken for granted for many years that greets us each morning and says good night to us each evening. It is the image we assume is reflected in the eyes of others. From this perspective, reacting so violently to the detachment from and loss of this image is understandable.

To use an exaggerated metaphor: when people lose a limb, their brains can have difficulty adjusting to the limb's absence and they experience "phantom limb syndrome." It's the body's neurological and perceptual reaction to a loss that does not match the physical reality; the brain continues to function as if the limb is still there. The absence of an image we connect to our identity—our face the way we choose to see it—is a loss that many women don't accept or can't absorb. Our instinctive reaction is to hold onto a familiar perception of ourselves, one that makes us feel comfortable and whole.

Even for a generation that grew up claiming we were about so much more, when faced with a sense that an aspect of our identity is being seized without consent, and that our choice to care or not is expiring, women panic. We may be unable to see clearly that changing looks means facing loss, not losing face.

## The Nature of Loss

You would think if looks didn't matter much to a woman, letting them go would be a breeze. Or, if looks mattered a lot, letting them go should be an extreme challenge. It's actually not so straightforward. We are not always conscious of how much our looks matter to us until we start losing them. Consequently, shifts in our self-image are more difficult until we learn to connect the dots.

Remember Leslie? She was the woman whose uh-oh moment came in the form of a panic attack during her birthday party at work. Until that moment, she took her good looks for granted, having used them as a treasured asset. Now she realized that no matter how much she worked at it, she had to deal with the changes in her looks that came with passing time. There was no going back to her "look," the one that she had assumed was how the rest of the world saw her. To move forward, she had to make a more positive pivot. She first had to acknowledge the meaning her appearance had in her life, historically, personally, and culturally. She told us, *"I was the daughter of two high-profile lawyers who had always kept our home and their lives in control. We didn't talk about it, but being 'well put together' was important, not only for them, but for us kids. I worked hard at everything, school, friendship, and my looks."*

We helped Leslie understand that being attractive in her youth had become linked to being in control. Control had been rewarded, at work and in the way she led her life. She felt she successfully maintained that connection throughout adulthood, but as her looks began to change, her control was challenged. To be out of control in any aspect of her life, she realized, meant disappointing herself, and, on some level, her parents as well. To let her looks change meant disconnecting from a positive image she held of herself, one that she relied on for many years. As she understood this, she also understood why an irrational concern set in with her uh-oh moment.

When Leslie faced letting go of her need for control, rather than her need for the static "look," which she knew on some level had to change, her panic eased. Sadness came in its place, which was more manageable and brought her closer to her deeper emotions. *"I realized I felt sad, as if I had to say good-bye to some part of myself I thought I always could control. But I began to calm down as I recognized that losing my youthful looks was more about leaving behind the kind of security I could find in other things in my life."* As Leslie understood the emotional and physical experience that was moving into the past, we helped her see she could make room for a more flexible self-image that could adjust more comfortably with the future.

It can be helpful to think back to the period or moments we felt most attractive. Sometimes it's when we fell in love or maybe it was one school dance where the right heels matched the right dress and people noticed.

•  •  •

**Sometimes feeling beautiful is associated to the times in our lives when we felt most secure and surrounded by people who loved us back. Often, we link these emotions and a physical state of attractiveness together. As a result, we may equate the desire to recapture these feelings with a wish to return to looking as we did at a certain age. Most often, we believe these memories lie somewhere in our youth.**

•  •  •

Jamie, the woman with the schoolgirl crush on a tennis instructor, couldn't see the connection between her changing looks and what was going on in her present-day life. They had never been her focus and she couldn't believe they were now. She didn't think there was much to mourn.

We asked Jamie about her family, her relationships, and developmental history to see if we could determine some clues to her midlife obsession. Jamie, unlike Leslie, said, *"I never saw myself as pretty. My mom and sister were the pretty ones. I was like my dad, athletic and bookish."* At first she was dismissive of the idea that her changing looks might be at all connected to her crush on her tennis coach, until we learned that her best times involved her father taking her out to play sports. *"My dad taught me to play tennis and golf. Maybe because he wanted company and my mom and sister weren't interested. It was probably the only time I had his undivided attention. I even remember he was willing to go to the pro shop and buy me tennis clothes that I'd try on for him. These were fun times. I was thin and in shape then. It's probably the only time I felt I was really special to him."* We wondered if these memories of looking and feeling special to her father were being revived as she was entering a new phase in life, the "empty next."

We reminded her that she had spoken of her husband's comments about her weight gain and suggested they may have set off her recent dismissal of him and fantasy of her coach. Although resistant to the idea that her appearance was at issue, she agreed it was likely that her wish to recapture emotional and physical images of herself may have been set off by the notion of losing her youth. Jamie let herself feel sad as she was reminded of her relationship with her father, who had passed away four years earlier. She began to realize how much she had been using sports to help her deal with her losses—not in itself a bad way to manage—and that her obsession was keeping her from moving on.

With awareness of how Jamie attached her self-image and well-being to aspects of her youth, she could begin to mourn a relationship that no longer existed, and focus more on the one that did. She entered couples counseling and is doing better, at tennis *and* family life. She recently told us that she encouraged her husband to take up tennis so he could join her on the court. Perhaps she was remembering the old adage "The couple that plays together . . . "

## Now the Good News: With Separation Comes a New Kind of Beauty

These connections recalled, identified, and then mourned, are clearly more difficult than the stories above imply. In her book, *Motherless Daughters*, Hope Edelman describes the processes of separation and letting go: *"Loss is our legacy. Insight is our gift. Memory is our guide."* Yet using these processes to move on takes time and emotional work. No doubt, enough has been said in popular culture about losing our buoyant young physical selves—the anxiety, fear, and dread of aging faces and bodies support entire advertising agencies. But the complex meaning behind separating from a youthful self-image is a critical psychological experience that has not been given its due.

Surprisingly, the process that leads to resolving this emotional transition was revealed to us as we noticed the parallels between leaving our modeling careers and aging. Having moved from that world, where appearance was so highly coveted, to become psychologists, where it had little discernible value, we had the opportunity to understand the mourning process that women face later in life. Here in magnified form, was a process all women faced, earlier and intensified. We had witnessed marginalization with colleagues considered "has-beens" at age 25, their agonizing emotional turmoil resulting from suddenly feeling detached from others' definitions of beauty.

We began to understand that as this detachment takes place, the losses are not only on the face or body, but to areas deeper within. It was the nature and personal meaning of their losses that determined the differences between those who were overwhelmed with dread in anticipation of ending their careers, and others who handled the transition more comfortably. Remember Alana, the model with insomnia?

Like many models we talk to, Alana said she not been conventionally pretty as a little girl. She described herself as *"too tall, gawky and unusual look-ing."* Her high-school boyfriend told her he saw her as exotic and suggested she try to make easy money modeling. With his encouragement she went to New York and was surprised that an agency took her on. *"Modeling meant the opportunity to escape my boring life in Kentucky, where I grew up tossed between my dad and mom who fought constantly."* Alana admitted that from her very first booking she loved the attention she received. *"I was thrilled to hear people 'ooh' and 'ah' over the long legs I thought were too skinny, my big eyes that I felt never fit my small face, and my thick hair that had rarely been washed as a kid."* We understood how being valued this way now filled Alana's reservoir in a way it had never been before. That is, temporarily.

The loss of youthful looks for Alana foreshadowed, as it does for many models, an intolerable emptiness. Although there are many exceptions, models like Alana often build careers trying to fill themselves with love and adoration, only to have these pleasurable feelings fall through the cracks of their foundation of self. Alana was terrified to return to memories of her past, yet back there is where we encouraged her to look. *"I was nothing before I modeled. My life was dull and pitiful. I go back now and shudder at what I could have become . . . like my hometown nobodies. I don't know what to do now. If I don't have my body and face to bring me what I'm used to, how will I get it? And I'm not just talking about the money!"*

Alana struggled to accept that she had connected her youthful image to many rewards she had come to take for granted, and that this could not always be the case. She had to recognize, although painful and unclear, that she needed to find other ways to fill her reservoir. She reluctantly agreed that the more she tried to hold onto staying perpetually young, the less attractive and loved she felt. It was only by letting go and mourning the loss of her model beauty—and all that was attached to it—that Alana could make room for other aspects

## GRIEVING THE LOSS OF YOUR YOUTHFUL LOOKS

• • •

Elisabeth Kübler-Ross describes five stages of mourning in her book *On Death and Dying.* Not surprisingly, these stages are very applicable to the process of loss women undergo at this stage of life. Take a look and see if they apply to feelings you have been having.

### Denial
You may be thinking, *"This can't be happening to me. I can't really be this old. My body can't be changing like this."*

### Anger
You may feel cheated. You may feel that you haven't hit the milestones you hoped for by this point. You may feel life isn't fair.

### Bargaining
You make deals with yourself, hoping that those deals will change the inevitable or ease the discomfort. Sometimes, unrealistic thinking may be involved. You may think, *"If I go to the gym every day, I'll get back my 21-year-old body,"* or *"If I get a face-lift, I won't have any more problems attracting men."*

### Depression
This is an emotional period during which you make peace with things as they are. You may feel fear, uncertainty, sadness, and regret—any or all of these—as you learn to focus on what you have rather than what you're losing.

### Acceptance
The is the ah-ha stage, when you have become objective enough to move forward and leave the past behind.

of herself to replace its undue importance. And with hard work, she did.

Interestingly, we found similar results among women from all walks of life. The differences among those at midlife who deal well with changing looks versus those that have a more difficult time largely relate to the nature and quality of the attachment to their looks. It is not about their actual appearance. And it is not, as it is for models, about prestige, money, or career. It is about the balance (or imbalance) beauty has with other aspects in one's life—youth, self-esteem, and self-image—the tumultuous troika strikes us all.

. . .

**The more we rely on youthful looks to feel good about ourselves, the more we hold on to them as we age, the less beautiful we ultimately feel. Letting go does not mean denying youth or repressing youthful memories. It means saying good-bye to make room for what comes next. A new definition of beauty can follow that is more flexible and occupies its place as one aspect among many others we value about ourselves.**

. . .

It may not be as clear to women whose looks obviously play a lesser role than Alana's did in her life, but her intensified version of loss highlights a process all women confront as we are faced with disconnecting from a youthful self-image. What is clear is that we can't recapture time. Alana couldn't continue to appear on the covers of fashion magazines or maintain contracts with cosmetics companies promoting smooth, unlined skin. Nor can we return to the self-image we once owned in our youths and may have associated with our own set of pleasures and rewards. The media might have us believe that any newfound rewards still available to us require recapturing youth, defying our age, and denying moving on, but in fact it requires the opposite. We need to mourn the passing of one chapter, letting go of what is no longer there, and move on to the next one.

Attractiveness that starts from within and moves outward is more reliable and less reactive to the world around us. If you are like other women who have followed our six steps, you have a newly found sense of beauty that no one, nor any culture, can take away. You recognize the reality of losses and experience gains as well. You may be saying good-bye to your youthful appearance, but there are aspects of beauty you never have to leave behind: the ability to smile with self-assurance, the confidence we have in who we are, our sensuality and openness to connecting with others.

Sophia Loren said regarding her changing looks, *"There is a fountain of youth: it is your mind, your talents, the creativity you bring to your life and the lives of people you love. When you learn to tap this source, you will truly have defeated age."* The bad news: few of us will ever be as gorgeous as Sophia Loren. The good news: there is no end to feeling attractive as a consequence of being fully engaged in life or being connected intimately with friends and family. Sharing kindness and exhibiting dignity and grace will contribute significantly to feeling beautiful for the rest of your life.

Let's face it: the way you once saw yourself is no longer the way you will see yourself as you look forward toward new definitions of beauty.

## Letting Go Requires Knowing What
## You Are Leaving Behind

- Describe that moment in time when you felt most appealing. See it as an image and describe it in words.

- Recall how you felt back then and what contributed to that feeling. Was it what you were doing at the time? Who you were with? The responses others had to you then?

- If you accept that you no longer have this youthful image, describe how you feel about the change? Would the change disappoint someone in your life? Is your connection to them challenged by the change?

- Imagine current moments in your life when you appear most natural, for example while taking a bath or when you first wake up in the morning. Is there anyone who might see you as attractive at these times, just as you are? What is it about you that they would like?

- Imagine these natural moments again and now use your inner eye to see yourself. Notice aspects of yourself that you find appealing— not based on the opinions of others.

- Using both what others like about you and what you found appealing about yourself, rewrite the internal dialogue that you hear in your head.

- With the knowledge that it is possible to let go of a youthful self-image and feel attractive at any age, how might you take care for yourself differently? It's never too late to enjoy how you look, so think of how to start making these changes now.

# SECTION III

Face a Changing Face

# chapter nine

· · ·

## Where the Valedictorian Meets the Prom Queen

*If all our women were to become as beautiful as the
Venus de Medici we should for a time be charmed, but
we should soon wish for variety and as soon as we
had obtained variety, we should wish to see certain
characteristics in our women a little exaggerated beyond
the then existing common standard.*

— Charles Darwin

## Meeting in the Middle

We've shared many vignettes of women at various stops along their internal journey toward external change. Some felt their appearance had played a large role in their lives. Others felt their looks barely mattered at all. We've learned that they eventually meet on the same playing field as they confront a common challenge: the undeniable fact of aging.

In this chapter, we will follow the step-by-step process of three women—Nancy, Katherine, and Jane—who represent different ends on the spectrum of the beauty experience. We tell their stories in detail, from their first uh-oh moments, through their gradual transformation to confidence in their changing skins. Dr. Diller's story is told as well. We think you'll identify with some aspect of these stories and find them helpful as you complete your own journey.

## Meet Nancy

Nancy is 5'3", weighs about 125 pounds, with green eyes and stylishly layered dark blonde hair. At first glance she could be Goldie Hawn without the giggle, the all-around girl-next-door all grown up. She is petite and in great shape. When we asked her how old she was, Nancy replied, *"I'm actually turning 50 next month. In 25 days exactly. Up until recently, people used to mistake me for being ten years younger. I just have, or had, that baby face. Can you believe in my 30s I was still being carded at bars? Obviously that doesn't happen anymore. I can't believe I have lived half a century! That's what 50 makes me think of."* She wasn't laughing when she said, *"Actually, I get a pit in my stomach as I think about my next birthday. I'm not sure what the pit is all about, but it's definitely not a good feeling."*

### The Role Looks Play in Nancy's Life—Cute and Fifty?

Nancy told us she couldn't remember a time when how she looked did not enter into her daily thoughts: *"I never thought of myself as beautiful. I'm what people call cute. I was into clothes growing up, loved flipping through fashion magazines. This really dates me, but my idols were the* Charlie's Angels *girls. I paid a lot of attention to what I wore, my haircuts and my makeup. And I've exercised most my life."*

She continued to describe how she saw herself: *"Everything about me is small: my nose, my hands and feet, and unfortunately, even my breasts. I make the most of what I've got. I was one of the first of my friends to wear push-up bras. Thank God for Victoria's Secret. I've always been good at putting myself together. I think I got that from my dad. He had real style. It's one of the few things he spent money on, expensive suits and classy silk ties. I'm the spitting image of my mom, but I'm more like my dad. I like choosing outfits before going to the office or out for the evening. It used to be more fun when I was younger. Now putting myself together is work and no matter what I wear, I don't look as good as I used to. Cute and 50 just don't go together."*

Nancy is by no means simply a cutie in the workplace. She is an executive in a multimedia advertising agency in Manhattan. She makes a good living, which is supplemented by child support she receives from her ex-husband. She left him 3 years ago after 20 years of marriage. He was unfaithful more than once and after years of dissatisfaction, she decided she'd had enough. They share joint custody of their two daughters, but her ex moved to Florida for business and now sees the girls only a couple times a year.

Nancy told us she realized she had become moody and irritable over the past few years. *"I am not myself,"* she said. Even her kids noticed. *"The other day they told me to go see a shrink! I used to blame my bad moods on my unhappy marriage, but my ex is basically out of my life, now that the girls are older. I wake up each day and feel like I'm on a treadmill. I go to work, come home, put some dinner on the table, take care of bills and after the girls go to bed, I do more work. I always bring projects home that I can't get done during the day. There never seems like enough time to do it all. I'm tired a lot."* Nancy sounded despondent and unable to target the source.

She continued, *"I want to meet someone, but I am too busy. Anyway, I usually don't have the energy to put myself together to go out. And even if I did, I'm too far out of the race."* We asked her what race she meant, and she said, *"I can't compete. There's no one left for someone like me, with two children, a body that is worn out and a face that looks tired. Who'd choose me over all these young girls? They're everywhere. I'm talking about the kind of girls that men like my ex hooked up with when we were married . . . still does, I suppose."*

Nancy sounded discouraged about her potential for another relationship and about her future in general, so we asked how long she had felt this way. She said, *"I think since my divorce, sometime in my mid-40s. Wow, I guess it's been a long time. For some reason turning 40 wasn't so bad, but when I entered my 40s, it was like I was in the next decade, headed toward my 50s. Fifty just is so old. I used to be a peppy person, laughed a lot, loved to be around people. But I've lost my zest lately. I don't feel like making the effort anymore. I look at myself each morning in the mirror and wonder what I have to look forward to. It's not like I've stopped thinking about my looks, but I don't get pleasure from them anymore. How will I ever meet someone?"*

Nancy's sadness seemed provoked by recent events and was out of sync with her usual optimism and positive attitude toward life. Some women say they have never been truly happy and aging can exacerbate their unhappiness. For others, like Nancy, sadness is an unfamiliar experience and doesn't fit with their image of who they are. This distinction is important to recognize, so that proper attention can be paid to the impact of precipitating events—like aging and changing looks—on midlife depression. You may be one of those women for whom looks played a small role in life and may find it hard to accept this idea. Or, like Nancy, you may be relieved that, with internal work, your attitude toward your future can change. Nancy was eager to move onward.

### Nancy's Uh-oh Moment: When the Pep Popped

We suggested that Nancy go back with us to the time she associated with having lost her "pep." We wanted to see if we could uncover a moment or series of moments that would help her understand what had provoked her depression. She said, *"I know things changed around my 41st birthday. I remember, because turning 40 wasn't bad, but being in my 40s was. I don't actually remember how I spent it. There was a lot going on in my life. It's all a blur. That's happening more these days. My friends tell me they feel the same way. Maybe it's our hormones. That's all I need now. Losing my memory along with the rest of my body! Maybe I just don't want to remember that time in my life."*

Hormones, memory loss, or the desire to forget: all three were likely playing roles in Nancy's uncharacteristic moodiness and we encouraged her to recall this phase in her life. *"From about 35 and into my 40s, I had been working very hard, trying to move up the ladder at my agency. It's known for being edgy and filled with young people, so I knew then I had to make my move up or I would lose my position. I remember there was this new VP of Sales who came on board a while back and I felt competitive in a way I hadn't before. I felt threatened the minute I met her. She was young, smart, and really pretty. And right at my heels. Just being around her, I felt my age.*" We asked Nancy to listen to how much value she had placed on beauty and youth and how this made her vulnerable as her appearance changed.

She went on: "*It wasn't an easy time, because it was around then I discovered my husband's first affair. He had been coming home late a lot. I didn't know it then, but looking back, there had been distance between us for a long time. He promised me he'd end the affair and we tried to work things out. But I never trusted him again. Meanwhile, it was about this time that the new girl came in my office. She walked in, looked at the picture I kept on my desk—it was of my girls when they were little—and she asked me if they were my grandkids! I almost fell off my chair. I guess you'd say that is when something hit me. I felt old and sad and things have never been the same.*"

This comment by Nancy's co-worker was the spark that set off her uh-oh moment. We helped Nancy acknowledge its meaning as a signal that her life and looks were changing, but reminded her that this event coincided with other upheavals as well. We explained that the comment provoked feelings that contributed to her moodiness and sense of hopelessness about her future and that it was not uncommon. We encouraged Nancy to open up about the emotions behind this blur of time, but first we had to identify the masks she wore.

### Nancy's Mask: Smoothing Those Bumps in Life?

"*There was a lot going on,*" Nancy continued, "*and I remember feeling a kind of anxiety that really hasn't left me. My husband's affairs came out in the open—yes, he had another. I think I just didn't want to see what was going on. There was a custody battle and I threw myself into my work. I thought I was coping all right,*" *but I started drinking more, especially when my life felt as if it was headed in a downward spiral. I wasn't always down, but now with my girls headed for college, it's depressing to think of my future, about looking and feeling so old."*

We helped Nancy begin to recognize she had been numbing herself through drinking and distracting herself with her work. But as with most masks, her efforts had not been successful. The feelings she had been having about the changes in her life—which had become evident since her uh-oh moment—were peering through the shield she wore. Preoccupied with her job and medicating herself using alcohol, she was masking underlying issues she needed to address.

Sure enough, Nancy responded, *"I complain all the time about how much I work, but I realize it's a great distraction. Being around these young people makes it easy to pretend to myself that I'm not 50 and helps me feel better temporarily. The problem is when they talk about stuff outside of work, like the late nights clubbing, staying out dancing and drinking, I realize how old I am. I wish I could go out with them, but I'm usually headed to bed when they're getting ready to go out. I'm asleep by 10 P.M. after I've had my glass of wine. I really don't belong with the people at work. I am not their age. Yet, if I look around, the people my age just seem so old!"*

Nancy confessed that she actually drank almost every evening, but didn't see herself abusing alcohol, a common reaction of midlife drinkers. She told us, *"I had some trouble with alcohol when I was in high school, but I got it under control by college. I use alcohol now because it smoothes the bumps in life. I probably should be careful, because I know it can get to be a habit with me. But I just don't know how to cope with this deep sadness I feel. I'm overwhelmed and out of control. It feels as if my emotions are running my life these days. I'm not used to that."*

### Nancy's Internal Dialogues: When the Words Pour Out

Nancy began to realize that both working and drinking too much were keeping her from coping effectively with the changes that had occurred in her physical and emotional life. As happens with many women, once the masks are identified and a window opens to what lies behind them, words come pouring out. We asked Nancy to listen to herself—her internal dialogues—to see if she could identify more clearly what was churning inside as a response to what was changing outside.

This is what she said, and what we heard: *"I don't like to think about how things are changing, how I don't look or feel the way I once did. I got used to a certain way of seeing myself in the world and everything seems to have changed."* We asked her to give us an example of that experience.

*"I used to walk into a room and kind of assume people would look at me and think I was cute. Now looking in the mirror I hear them saying just the opposite. I guess I'm just not cute anymore and I don't think I can attract guys the way I did. That's really depressing."*

We asked her to talk more about how her changing looks may have affected her relationships with men. *"At first, after my divorce, I felt free and excited about meeting new men. I even enjoyed dating, but that didn't last long. I think on some level my husband's affairs took their toll on my trust and on my self-esteem."* Nancy told us that her dates didn't lead anywhere. Self-doubt began to creep in. *"Now, with my face changing, I just don't feel like dating is fun anymore. I've had some Botox. It helped, for a while, but I still haven't found myself feeling that much better. I feel pretty hopeless about anyone ever being attracted to my body, especially since I find it so unappealing."*

We said her openness was a good beginning, as was recognizing that she'd been running from her feelings for some time. We told her that denial and avoidance of what we experience at this time in our lives often shows up on our faces in a pinched and negative way. And that those who confront, absorb, and cope with these emotions have faces that show a relaxed confidence, often seen by others as attractive. Nancy began to listen to her own internal dialogues and through them exposed important themes about the role her looks played in her life. To deal more effectively with the impact, she needed to explore these themes further. We suggested that Nancy look back at her history, to understand better why natural but discomforting physical changes were bothering her in the way they did, which is where she headed next.

### Nancy's Family History: Is Home Where the Hurt Was?

Nancy shared information about her family and growing up. *"Like I said, I am more like my dad, though I look a lot like my mom. I didn't have a good relationship with her. My mom was considered very pretty in her day, long and lean and stylish. Dad used to say I was a cute version of her. My mom and I just didn't get along. Sometimes I think we competed for my dad's attention. He paid a lot of attention to me. He came to watch my cheerleading practices. He's the one who took pictures, the only ones I have from those days. I remember being happy when we were all living together. I was their only child. I think my mom would have liked to have more, but my dad made me feel that having one was just the right number."* As we listened carefully to Nancy's family history, we understood that her self-confidence and sense of appeal were likely rooted in positive experiences she had in the context of her intact family, especially with her father. *"When I was 14 and my parents got divorced, I wanted to live with my dad, but I wasn't given that choice. I missed him a lot, especially when he moved south."* We asked Nancy to tell us more about that phase of her life. *"Well, it was messed up by the divorce. I had a lot of friends, but I got into some trouble . . . drugs, lots of drinking. I was with the cool kids; at least that's how I remember it. And I always had a boyfriend. I wanted to shut my mother out, and drinking and boys helped me through that time."* Nancy's self-image in adolescence was challenged by the changes that occurred at home and the changes that were occurring in her body. Her current coping measures could be traced to those she used then. She went on: *"It wasn't that great visiting my dad. He had a new wife—he remarried when I was 16. My mom never met anyone else, though she tried. I guess I was jealous of my dad's new wife and so was my mom. She blamed my stepmom for everything. My dad had more children and I liked having siblings, but was jealous of them too, or at least of the attention he gave them. I envied their happy lives. It was a really tough time. I was moody then too but it's easy to see why."*

We asked Nancy to consider that the changes she was experiencing now may be reviving old feelings, especially ones from her adolescence. Nancy felt intrigued by the similarity between the two tumultuous times and wanted to explore the parallels further, so we did. She told us, *"When my parents divorced, everything changed."* She described how she saw life fundamentally different from that time on. We suggested that she had been seeking the stability she felt she had lost ever since and that this old yearning kept her from viewing her present choices more clearly.

Nancy began to recognize that she was again using alcohol to anesthetize herself from emotional pain, as she had in her teens, and how unhelpful that was. *"Back then, there was no one I could really turn to other than my friends. We all drank too much. It was just what we did. My parents were fighting and I got caught in the middle. My stepmom actually helped me keep from getting into serious trouble with alcohol, but I just wanted to get away from the whole situation."*

She continued: *"Things got better when I left for college and I met Bobby, my now ex-husband. I got my cheery self back again, stayed away from alcohol. Back then he was on the football team. I was a cheerleader. I was in a good phase, well liked, passing grades, and a popular boyfriend. Seems so long ago."*

What followed were several years of positive memories, two children, working hard at jobs and raising a family. For a while, Nancy believed she had it all. The troubles in her marriage and the loss of solid footing at her job changed everything. She entered a phase of life in which she felt stuck. Set off by these life events, it left Nancy feeling and looking old and preoccupied with no solution in sight. Clearly, she was in a crisis and it was time to face it.

*Nancy's Shift: Letting Go, Moving Forward,
and Making an About-Face*

First we wanted Nancy to clearly recognize that her appearance had played a significant role in her self-esteem for most her life. We reminded her that this was not unusual for women of her generation and was in part why the changes in her looks had such an impact on her now. She was interested: *"On a scale of one to ten, where do I fall?"* A hard question to answer, since feelings are not easily calibrated, but we understood Nancy's desire to gain a tangible and manageable way to understand herself. We told Nancy that a connection between appearance and self-esteem was difficult to quantify or reduce to a number, but that she was at the higher end of the scale. She nodded as if she already knew this, and said, *"So how does that help me and what do I do next?"*

We took this opportunity to tell Nancy that many women wanted to know exact steps to follow, a time line and road map to guide them toward change. We told her we wished there was a clear and exact prescription, like taking a pill twice a day, that would lead to feeling beautiful as we age. But it didn't work that way—even if our culture would have us believe otherwise—and that looking backward, inside and out would help her move forward. We told her we would help her use her insights to put change into practice, what we call the "working through" process in psychotherapy.

We told Nancy that her history revealed that her positive, upbeat sense of herself had developed while her family was still intact and that her self-image was nurtured by a strong, positive relationship with her father. Her father had clearly shared his delight with his "one child," and this emotional backdrop had been very important in her definition of herself. We described her "reservoir" as filled, in part, with the physical qualities she identified as cute, and in part by her dad's adoration and interest. Based on this relatively solid foundation, Nancy was able to maintain a positive sense of self for many years. But being unable to comfortably identify with her mother, and the poor relationship between her mother and father, left fault lines in her reservoir. She began to understand that this was what lay behind her difficulties with present-day relationships and with her vulnerable sense of self as she aged.

We described further the effects of Nancy's turbulent adolescence in her life now. Her parents' divorce was traumatic, not only because the process was filled with open hostility and disruption, but because it came during a difficult emotional time in her life. We emphasized that Nancy's world was shaken during her teens and so was her sense of self. Additional insult came with her dad choosing another woman. Even though Nancy acknowledged her stepmom as a positive influence, she recognized that she still felt displaced and vulnerable to competition during this sensitive adolescent phase. Her general positive character was left vulnerable to rejection and competition, a scenario confronting her again at midlife.

As we delved into Nancy's history and identified the roots of her vulnerabilities later in her life, she gained a greater sense of control. She began to use knowledge to fill in the gaps. For example, instead of being confused by her feelings toward men, Nancy used her family history to recognize why approval by men was so compelling to her sense of well-being. Every glance her way, compliment, and nod of recognition repeated the positive experiences she recalled, but lost, with her father. She said, *"I can see now why I may have been so attached to my husband. I was always seeking his approval while we were married and even after his first affair."* We suggested that she felt compelled to undo the hurt she experienced when her father left the family, by proving to herself that her husband would be different. She seemed to convince herself that she could stop his straying habits if she could only be the cute young girl he fell for in college. Unaware of her compelling need for his—and her father's—loyalty, Nancy felt reflexively driven to remain youthful looking, with little success in reaching her goal.

We helped Nancy see that with her uh-oh moment, not only did she face being viewed as older, she saw herself as her mother—abandoned and left alone. Our work now was to help

Nancy recognize that her aging did not have to replicate her mother's experience and that getting older didn't necessarily mean being alone. The process of Nancy's shift was clear to us, yet we knew that making the shift would require looking more honestly at her past and doing hard emotional work to let it go.

The masks Nancy used to protect her from these feelings were obvious to her. She knew she had been drinking to numb herself, but it was less obvious that she was also working too hard and that too was keeping her from moving forward. Now that she was beginning to face her feelings, we helped her recognize that she no longer needed to work so hard to cover them. We gave strong support for her to stay away from alcohol, and as she had done before, Nancy stopped drinking altogether. Breaking that habit was actually a welcome relief for Nancy, since she had known the positive outcome of having stopped once before. Breaking the work habit was harder, but she said, *"When I realized work was covering up other stuff, I also realized I was making more work for myself that I didn't really have to do."* With clarity over the role work played to mask other feelings, she began to relax about it and even enjoyed the greater security she actually had at her job.

The hardest part for Nancy, and for many women, was letting go and mourning. Nancy felt deep sadness as she recognized that to move on, she needed to grieve the loss of the youthful positive connection she once had with her father and accept that she might never experience that kind of connection again. It's easy to see that Nancy may have warded off these painful feelings by unwittingly trying to re-create being daddy's special girl through her present relationships with men. These feelings of loss were not easy to face, but face them she did.

Our personal histories differ, but all of our past experiences weave in some way with our present. This is especially relevant when we're attempting to understand the true impact of the emotional events in our lives. Once Nancy began to recognize and mourn the sense of self that she had attached to her past, she began to make room for a new connection that was more suited to her present-day life. With that mourning, Nancy's fears about her changing looks started to ease. Instead of holding on tightly to an old image, the only one she thought made her appealing, Nancy shifted her focus to a more realistic one—an image she could enjoy even as she aged.

It's worth noting that not only did it become clear to Nancy that her fear of aging meant losing the sense of worth she had connected to her youth, but that this connection was being reinforced by the culture she lived in. Especially in her work environment, it was easy for her to fall victim to the pressure to stay looking young to feel attractive. We helped her look inward to a self that she had more control over. The imbalance for most of her life—that her appeal was strongly based on her physical attractiveness—was brought into balance as she gained a greater sense of her value as a hard-working single mom who had done a fine job supporting herself and caring for her family. Instead of devaluing her life, she began to elevate a host of true qualities that could stay with her forever.

As Nancy increasingly accepted her attractiveness as based on more than a former image of her physical self, she was ready to move on.

## Meet Katherine

On the scale Nancy referred to, Katherine was on the other end of the spectrum. She told us, *"For as long as I can remember, I have never put much emphasis on my appearance."* She had a natural, outdoorsy look, a healthy complexion, and most often wore no makeup. She said her best traits were her straight white teeth and thick curly hair, which she began to let gray the prior year. Katherine is 53, stands at 5'8", and, according to her own judgment, is "40 pounds overweight."

### The Role Looks Play in Katherine's Life: More Important Things to Worry About

Katherine told us she had gained 60 pounds during her third and last pregnancy and had not really focused on losing the extra baby weight. She hoped, as after having her other children, it would just fall off eventually. *"I gained more this time because, bottom line, I let myself go. I was working, taking care of my two sons and feeling nauseated all day long. I ate lots of crackers. I mean lots, like boxes of Ritz crackers. They're delicious and filled with fat! But they kept me from being sick and I guess I just haven't gotten back onboard with good eating. I plan to. I know it's not good to carry this much weight. And I feel like a horse, not my old self. Or maybe this is my new self, I can't decide."*

Now that she was on extended leave from the research job she had held for ten years, Katherine hoped to take better care of herself. Mostly she wanted to spend time with her three children and a little more time on herself. Both she and her husband were delighted that their last child was a girl, giving their sons a sister. They felt lucky to be parents and were devoted to their children, although at times they wished they had started their family earlier.

About beauty, Katherine told us, *"I had always been more invested in other things, like being smart, doing well in school, relationships, and my family. Growing up I had interests that mattered more to me than the latest fashions. Even now, I'll always start the* Times *with the Week in Review and Arts and Leisure sections before getting to the Style section, which I often throw out. As it is, I don't have much time to read with the three kids, but I surely wouldn't waste my free time reading about other people's styles. Maybe I just don't get what's important about clothes and makeup. Clothes seem like a hassle to me, something I have to deal with. When I was working, I used to wish my job had a uniform, so I wouldn't have to think about it. As it is, now I have my home uniform . . . a T-shirt and sweats."*

Clearly, Katherine's looks were not her focus, but she was more than happy, and maybe a bit proud, to share that fact.

She continued, *"My mom is a retired history teacher and my dad is a doctor, so academics took precedence over almost everything else. And it didn't help being smack in the middle of two brothers and having a little sister we all treated like the baby. She was much younger and more into girl stuff. Actually no one really talked about girly things, not even my mom, except in a devaluing way, like how silly it all was."* So Katherine never bothered much with her face and body, even as an adolescent. Katherine, and women like her, grew up contending that looks were *"superficial concerns for superficial girls,"* remaining off their radar screen as they developed into women of substance.

Mostly, Katherine nurtured other aspects of herself for her source of self-esteem and she left her looks to take care of themselves. It was only recently, as she was noticing difficulty taking off her pregnancy pounds, that her appearance seemed to be finding its way into her thoughts. She said, *"I notice my face and body changing and am a bit frustrated that I can't lose weight. I could let it all go, or I could do something about it, but that takes time and effort. I don't even like that I have to think about it, but I guess I do, because this weight thing is beginning to get to me."*

### Katherine's Uh-oh Moment: The Mirror That Doesn't Lie

Katherine said, *"I know on some level, the changes I see in the mirror creep into my mind, but I fight putting any weight— ha ha—into my concerns. I'm the kind of person who never gets on a scale, manicures seem like the biggest waste of time and I get my hair cut at the local barber. I honestly think I've never set foot in Henri Bendel or Saks and I've lived in New York all my life. I have been taking second looks in the mirror lately. I have to admit, I don't like what I see. I just don't want to become the kind of woman my brothers always made fun of. That's more my sister. Not me."* In spite of herself, Katherine acknowledged that her looks mattered, even if it pained her to admit it.

With a little coaxing, Katherine shared a vulnerable moment during a recent exchange with her husband. He had suggested they take a vacation together away from the children, back to St. John where they honeymooned. The idea of a second honeymoon, unfortunately, led to serious second thoughts. *"At first I thought it would be great, but the more I imagined myself spending time on a beach, the less sure I was about taking the time from the kids or exposing my skin to that much sun. Actually, I wasn't sure what I felt, but he insisted it would be great for us and made reservations. I didn't really want to tell him—and I usually tell him everything—that what I was thinking about was how awful I'd feel in a bathing suit. I just felt too stupid and ashamed to admit that to him."*

Katherine searched through her drawers and discovered two swimsuits that fit her a couple of kids ago. So she went shopping, an experience that turned out to be both alien and unpleasant. *"One of the saleswomen brought me a two-piece and I nixed that right away. No way I'd expose the stretch marks and folds of extra skin on my belly. I really wish I didn't care, but I couldn't imagine myself bare bellied. Then she brought me these new styled tankinis, the ones that cover a lot but are stylish. When I tried one on and looked at myself, I felt like a 50-year-old trying to look 30. It just didn't work. In the end, I bought a suit that looked like the one-pieces my grandmother used to wear. I realized I wouldn't like anything I tried on since it wasn't the suit I didn't like, it was how I looked. No suit was going to make me feel like I used to. I never was a bathing beauty, but at least I looked in shape. I ended up telling my husband that I just didn't think I could do a trip like this now, that the school year was starting and it was probably not a good time to travel. I wasn't surprised by his confusion since I had been talking about needing a break. But I didn't want to get into explaining why I really didn't want to go."*

Clearly this was an uh-oh moment for Katherine, who had been successful up until then in keeping her appearance in the background. But, like all women, there is an inevitable moment when we are confronted with the changes that come with age. A paradoxical pull emerged with Katherine's uh-oh moment, as it does for many women whose looks have not been their priorities: *"If I care about my looks, I feel embarrassed, but if I don't take care of them, I'll still feel embarrassed."* Unable to find her way out, Katherine felt stuck. Stuck enough to cancel a potentially enjoyable vacation. A smart woman in so many other ways, Katherine was unable to make a wise decision for herself.

### Katherine's Mask: The "I Don't Care" Offense as Defense

We encouraged Katherine to see her confusing experience about her looks as part of a cultural norm for other women too. We told her that paradoxical feelings about beauty often caught them by surprise. She confirmed, *"This was not supposed to matter to me. I have these great kids, this wonderful husband, and a good job. I feel as if I shouldn't be feeling upset and out of control of my life, but I know I don't like what I feel. I always thought of myself as so young. I know I'm in my 50s, but I've never stopped thinking of myself as in my 30s. I guess I hadn't really looked at myself in the mirror in so long I could keep hold of that illusion. What I saw that day in the bathing suit shop was not what I remember myself to be. I really don't know how this happened—or maybe I do, but I haven't wanted to focus on it."*

Katherine, like many accomplished women, didn't anticipate that her aging face and body would disturb her and so believed she needed to keep these feelings at bay. It's the "dare I care" syndrome. Katherine was able to mask her uncomfortable feelings by fortifying their lack of importance relative to other things in her life. She said, *"While I was having my three children and working so hard, I really couldn't think about anything else. My kids are everything to me. It's how I justify working so hard. My husband and I wanted a girl after having two boys. And being able to get pregnant again made me feel young."*

Katherine managed to avoid concerns about aging and her changing body by focusing on other, loftier values. She also added that, *"being a science researcher and an older mother of three made it easy to neglect my appearance. The people I saw daily at my lab and in the playground made my looks seem unimportant to me."* At least until her mask was uncovered and her emotions emerged more clearly.

## Katherine's Internal Dialogues: Looks Come Out of Hiding

*"If I let my thoughts go, I guess with what you call 'internal dialogues,' I'd have to say I actually think about how I look more than I'd like to admit,"* said Katherine. *"I feel differently about my looks now than in the past in that I used to take them for granted. I see myself looking tired and try to convince myself that when I find the time, which will probably be never, I'll get around to putting some cream on—like that Retin A stuff I hear about—or make an appointment with a dermatologist. I can't really talk to anyone, because no one in my family thinks about these things. Actually, my sister does, but I'd never admit my issues to her. My mother never took care of her looks and my brothers couldn't care less. Anyway, after we didn't go on that vacation, I found myself thinking that I'll never wear a bathing suit again and that saddens me. I used to be so carefree about my body. Not that I thought I was a beauty queen—my sister was the pretty one. But, I guess I just didn't care that much. Now I feel ashamed of the cellulite, the veins I see on my legs, stuff I never thought I'd care about."*

Aging does not discriminate. Women with Ph.D.s and GEDs do it. Wallflowers, who always expected to stay there, do it. Brainiacs who master all other equations do it. Prom queens who never thought they would do it. Aging isn't the problem. It's how we deal—or don't deal—with it that is. As Katherine opened up more, her indifference to her appearance seemed to mask some of the more complicated feelings she had regarding her mother's lack of focus on Katherine's femininity.

*"It's as if it's all catching up to me and I don't want to care, but I do. I feel silly even talking about it. My sister invites me to get pedicures and facials with her, but I just don't enjoy them. I wish*

*now I had paid attention to some things, like keeping my weight in control. My sister is in great shape, but I think she works at her body too much. She went in the opposite direction my mother and I did. My body feels out of control and I feel there's no going back. Even sexually, I don't feel like I used to. I'm not comfortable taking off my clothes. How weird is that? My husband and I don't have much sex these days. I say it's because of the kids being around all the time or that I'm just too tired. But it's also because I don't feel sexy in this body. I think that's sad. If I really am honest with myself, I think it's sad that the changes I've let happen and the changes that are happening to me are affecting my life in ways I wish I could control. Instead, I'm eating more and feeling a bit hopeless."*

Katherine's internal dialogues confirm our belief that we all meet on the same playing field as our looks change. Women from both ends of the beauty spectrum feel out of control, desire to hold on, and seek solutions.

### Katherine's Family History: Smart about Everything Else

We asked Katherine to take us back to her youth, to see if we could use an understanding of her developmental history to help her move forward through midlife more successfully. We already knew from things she told us that her family showed little interest in activities and behaviors typically associated with femininity. It made it difficult for Katherine to incorporate feminine values into her self-image. It was not that she questioned her sexual identity, but feeling pride about being female was complicated. We asked her to elaborate on her adolescent years, since we knew it was during that time that her sexual and feminine identity would have been emerging.

She said, *"Being a girl, next in line after two athletic brothers, was tough in my house. I remember I once took an ace bandage from my brother's sports bag and wrapped it around my breasts to keep them from jiggling around. Hard to imagine when now you see young teenage girls getting implants. I wanted mine to be flatter, more like those volleyball players you see at the Olympics who seem to have no* breasts. *Mine weren't gigantic, but when they popped, I was embar-rassed."* She told us she bought her first bra at age 13 without her mother. Her younger sister was different. *"She made a big deal over getting her period and buying nice lingerie. I thought she was such a baby most of the time. I have to say, I probably didn't make it easy for her either. Only recently have I thought of asking her for some advice. About beauty stuff."*

Katherine said she grew up focused on her schoolwork and on playing sports. She tried hard to be like her brothers, who she looked up to even though they teased her a lot, especially about being a girl. We asked her to tell us more about that. *"One time they took my bra out of my room. I remember, it was this big white ugly thing and they ran around the house swinging it and wearing it around their necks. I was totally humiliated, but I remember acting as if I didn't care. I ran to my mom, but she wasn't much help. She told me to ignore them. Her suggestion was that when they made fun of me, to put my head in a book and read. I think that's what I did. I read a lot and still do. And I ate. I gained a lot of weight during my teens. I guess that's similar to what I do now. I better figure this stuff out before my daughter gets to her teens."* We agreed that it would be a good idea, not just for her daughter, but for her sons as well and their attitude toward female sexuality.

And what about the person Katherine would have naturally turned to for beauty and feminine advice growing up? *"My mom and I were close, but we never talked about female stuff. She just seemed embarrassed when I asked her questions. Maybe that's why I was eager to have a girl, to see if I could do things differently with her."* Katherine told us she had been a tomboy and even to this day almost never wore skirts or dresses. Nor did her mother. *"My mom is completely gray now and has looked old for as long as I remember. Even in pictures of her when she was younger, she looked like the librarian type. I don't like to think of myself that way, but I guess without realizing it, I'm becoming her. I don't want to, if I really think about it. Are you telling me I don't have to be?"* We told Katherine it's never too late to get smart about beauty.

Katherine admitted that after the bathing suit incident, she found herself sneaking peeks at the book *How Not to Look Old* while browsing at her local bookstore. Ultimately she bought it, albeit making sure it remained hidden between the history and travel books. *"Funny,"* she said, *"it reminded me of how I'd sneak romance novels between the other books I brought home from the library when I was young. I only read them late at night when everyone else went to sleep."* Now Katherine said she did the same with her new self-help book, reading it in the bathroom and sneaking glances at herself in the mirror every so often as she found herself relating to what she read. *"It was a book with an insulting title and I felt ridiculous for reading it, but it did have a helpful hint or two. I actually made an appointment with my dentist. I've even thought about cutting bangs. I can't believe I'm telling you this! I didn't even tell my husband."* Again, Katherine acknowledges that she didn't want him or anyone to know she cared enough about her changing looks to do anything about them.

*Katherine's Shift: Time to Face It*

Katherine started her shift by having to acknowledge, with less shame and embarrassment, that her appearance held some value. Recognizing the role beauty plays in our sense of self—and the impact of our changing looks—is the first step women need to take on their journey to a new perspective. In certain ways, this first step was harder for Katherine than for Nancy, who already knew that beauty mattered. While Nancy's transition required a loosening of the close tie between her appearance and her self-esteem, Katherine first had to recognize that there was any connection at all. Katherine didn't have to mourn an image of herself as young and pretty. She had to mourn aspects of her femininity that had failed to be nurtured.

To identify and own her true reactions to her changing looks, we asked Katherine to carefully consider the paradoxical pulls she felt that made this acknowledgment so difficult. We also asked her to be aware of how these conflicting pulls began in her childhood and had continued to be reinforced in her work culture. Without this understanding, women like Katherine are confused when they are suddenly caught by feelings that seem to come out of nowhere and make little sense. We told Katherine that she was among many women who felt, *"If looks were not supposed to matter, why do we care as we see changes in them as we age?"* Katherine worked to let her looks find their place in her identity, so she could move on. To let go and make a shift, she needed to know from where she was moving and from what she was letting go.

Looking at Katherine's coping measures, when her body changed during adolescence, helped her further understand the difficulties she encountered managing her changing looks now. Keeping herself a shapeless girl and overeating during her teens were ways of coping (or trying to) that she was reenacting now at midlife. Failing to lose her pregnancy weight, allowing herself to lose interest in sex, and neglecting her appearance kept her from dealing more directly with the feelings about her changing looks.

Katherine's uh-oh moment, when she canceled her trip with her husband, was a reminder of the shame and embarrassment she had over her body years ago. Instead of wrapping herself in her brother's ace bandages as she did in adolescence, now she felt like hiding behind a "grandma" bathing suit. She couldn't experience pleasure in her own body, or even work with it to feel better. Instead she kept from looking. We encouraged her not only to look, but to realize no one was making fun of her anymore.

Once Katherine allowed her looks to have some meaning to her, with greater dignity and less shame, she felt the ambivalence that often comes with that recognition. On one hand she began to enjoy renewed possibility about the pleasure that comes with being female, but also the regret that often comes when women recognize for the first time that they have minimized this pleasure most of their lives. For example, Katherine, who had rejected and devalued some of her sister's feminine pleasures, told us, *"I never realized how nice it feels to be pampered at a spa, until I finally allowed my sister to take me to one. It wasn't until this year that I realized that a massage could be so relaxing. Decadent, but so good for me. And who would have thought a pedicure could actually make me feel pretty? I used to hide my toes and scoffed at women who wasted time at these salons. It actually upsets me to think that I never indulged in any of these fun activities, especially when I had more time. I didn't let myself. Instead, I let my looks go and now it's so hard to get back. I'm hooked on neck massages and want to work out more. I'm still not sure about the pedicure-and-manicure habit quite yet."*

Katherine's mourning required not only feeling some regret over losing her chance to enjoy youthful femininity, but also disconnecting from an identity she developed in her family. Paying attention to her looks meant joining her sister, feeling more like her sister than her brothers, and letting her appearance share the stage with the other values her family and work had reinforced. Mourning is harder for women like Katherine, because they don't anticipate the feelings that come with changing looks. It requires recognizing lost time and lost opportunities as looks matter for the first time.

Katherine had to separate from the proud image she had of herself as being above the silliness attributed to femininity. But the more she was able to let go of that connection, the more free she felt to make her own choices. She could enjoy the fact that she was tall, strong, and feminine, and embellish her appearance if she chose. Instead of avoiding the pleasures of femininity, they came under her control. Not only did she join her sister for occasional massages, she had her hair styled by a hairdresser and even enjoyed buying some fashionable handbags. *"Maybe I found these indulgences late in life, but it's the first time I've actually enjoyed some of the things women can do that men can't. I never thought that buying colorful handbags or scarves as something women indulge in that men don't. I always thought of what we can't do that men can! Funny it's taking me so long, but I guess it's never too late, nor will I ever be too old to buy a nice purse."*

Like Katherine, we've met many women who get stuck in the need to elevate themselves above the superficiality of being "girly," but then deprive themselves of the "how lovely to be a woman" stage. Katherine admitted, *"I didn't work hard to get a Ph.D. just to end up caring about my appearance . . . but looking back, it's kind of upsetting that I didn't let myself care at all. Now that I am beginning to, it feels too late. I'm just beginning to realize I can care about who will be our next president or if our earth is overpopulated even if I look after my appearance. I think I bought into the idea that being a feminist meant being anti-looks. Hey, even Gloria Steinem cares how she looks!"* The more Katherine talked, the more comfortable she felt about trying to find a good balance.

Recently, Katherine showed up at a barbecue her brother was having for the family, wearing a bit of makeup and a new stylish haircut. Her husband told her she looked great, but her brothers made a big deal over the changes. She said, *"I guess I should have expected it. My younger brother asked me if I had borrowed my sister's lipstick. My other brother just said, 'What's this about?' implying there had to be some distasteful reason for my caring. Fortunately, I had begun to understand it was our family's issue, not mine, that made them uncomfortable with the whole subject of beauty."* With less shame over the role her physical appearance could play in her life, Katherine in fact began to enjoy taking better care of herself, without denying the importance of other aspects. We helped her see that she didn't need to "fit" into any particular corner of the playing field, but rather that she had choices and the freedom to care for, and see herself as, an attractive *and* smart woman.

## Meet Jane

Jane represents a group of women often omitted in the books and articles about beauty and aging. Having felt unattractive most of her life, Jane—and women like her—dismisses the very subject of beauty. It's not that they don't care or belittle those who do. They've simply been on the sidelines of the playing field as long as they can remember, so they don't think it is worth getting into the game now. We don't see it quite the way Jane does, which is why we include her story and encourage women who feel like her to read on. We've found that when we persuade all women to talk openly about looks, they not only can change their perspective about beauty and aging, but their stories are of much greater—and wider—interest than they expect.

Jane is 44, average height and weight. She has never married and supports herself working as an assistant at the local ASPCA. She loves animals and she loves her job. The first thing she told us about herself was that, *"I feel at my age, I am lucky that I do the kind of work that I enjoy and that I'll be able to do it for a long time. Sometimes I can't believe I get paid to work at something I would do anyway. I've taken care of animals all my life."* Presently, she has two dogs and one cat of her own. Her "babies," she called them. At other times she has cared for up to five animals in her small apartment in Brooklyn. Jane is not the spinster who will end up in a small apartment with 100 cats. She is a lively, engaged, caring, nice-looking woman who simply felt she missed out on one aspect of life and that it's too late to climb aboard.

### The Role Looks Play in Jane's Life: Who Looks at My Looks?

Since our interview was about aging and women's self-image, we directed Jane to not only talk about her work, but about her appearance as well. She laughed and said, *"Okay, but there's not much to say."* Then, mocking herself, she added, *"I don't know which came first, my name or looking the part, but I've always considered myself a plain Jane. Not exactly 'Ugly Betty,' more like 'Not Pretty Jane.'"* Unlike Katherine, who found comfort in elevating herself above talking about or caring about her looks, Jane devalued herself instead.

*"No one in my family is especially attractive. Maybe it's in our genes."* She continued, *"The picture I have of myself now is not that different than when I was a kid. I had ears that stuck out, a big space between my front teeth, boring brown hair that had a mind of its own, and a kind of chunky body. I wasn't weird looking. No one made fun of me, or anything like that. I was just nothing much to write home about. As I grew older, not much changed. My teeth improved with braces, I grew big boobs, and I got bad skin. I'm a junk food lover, so I'm sure that didn't help. The worst thing about how I look is my skin. I had a bad case of acne in my teens and it has never fully gone away. You'd think I'm too old to get pimples, but I'm one of those lucky few! Just joking . . . maybe I'll still grow out of them. I try not to think about it much. And I don't wear makeup to cover it, since it only calls attention to my face."*

We told Jane we understood that her looks were not a topic she was used to discussing, but we asked her if she even noticed that others did care. *"Sure. It's not like I don't think about other people's looks. I'm a* People *magazine addict and I love* Entertainment Tonight. *But, I don't like to think much about my own appearance. I guess it makes me think too much about ending up alone. I don't look forward to growing old by myself, but what can I do? I've never been in a long-term relationship—a couple of dates and that's the end of it. Men just don't find me interesting."*

We wondered, given Jane's perspective, how changes in her looks as she aged affected her. *"I don't think aging and how my looks are changing matter much to me. It's more about no one having bothered to look in the first place and now, for sure no one will. I see the changes and it reminds me that I'm getting older and that I'll end up all alone."* Again she turned the conversation to her work, clearly a place of comfort and source of self-esteem. *"At least I have my animals and a job. Some women don't have that. I look at these women who seem so desperate to look young or search for men as company or to be noticed and do crazy things to get it."* We agreed and told her that it was true, that in these ways, she truly was fortunate to have meaningful work in her life. But then she added, *"In some ways, having felt almost invisible all my life makes aging less painful and becoming even more invisible less painful, I suppose. I don't feel sad about losing something I never had."*

Jane's poignant words of resignation were similar to those we heard over and over among women who claimed to have never felt attractive during their lives. We suggested that Jane let her thoughts about aging be spoken out loud, even if her focus wasn't on her changing appearance. In spite of Jane's pessimism, we were convinced if she listened carefully to her own internal dialogues, we could help her alter her vision of herself. Although each of us approaches our changing looks with a different script, rewriting is possible for all women.

We asked Jane more questions about her reactions to her changing looks. Had she actually had an uh-oh moment she may have not been aware of? Were there feelings about her appearance lying near the surface? Did she have masks that kept her from approaching issues about her looks that we could talk about in more hopeful terms than she had in the past? We were convinced that Jane could see aging as an opportunity to enter a playing field that had finally been leveled, rather than a continuation of what had come before. So, we moved on and inward, and Jane was willing.

### Jane's Uh-oh Moment: Not a Party Animal

Intrigued by the notion of "equal opportunity" as women got older, Jane opened up more about her internal experience of aging. She described an event in her life that she felt might be related to our topic, although at the time, she remembers dismissing it as just her way of dealing with life. *"There was a Christmas party last winter at the ASPCA. We were involved in planning it for weeks, the food, the decorations. I usually don't like parties but I wanted to be there, in part for the animals, but also because the people who work there are like family. The morning before the party I realized I wanted to wear something a bit different than my usual work clothes. I never took much time to think about what to wear to work. Everything just gets soiled and besides, animals don't care! But people were bringing their spouses and families, so it did cross my mind to take time to dress up, maybe wear some makeup. I realized I didn't have one dress that wasn't about five years old and my makeup was dried out.*

*"It was when I went to a department store to buy a dress and one of these sales people stopped me to sit at a makeup counter. That did it. I could see my bad skin in that magnified mirror, black pores and now, new brown spots I hadn't seen before. It was horrible. I don't ever look that close. I went home and decided to just go in my usual clothes with a little makeup. No one even noticed. But I did. During the party, I spent most of my time with the animals and I know it's silly, but I kept saying to myself, they think I'm wonderful and don't care about my looks. I knew I would be alone the rest of my life, but I have them."* Jane told us she went home from the party early and spent New Year's Eve, as she had many times before, watching the ball drop on TV with her "babies."

### Jane's Masks: Work Hard and Make 'Em Laugh

Jane learned to develop ways to keep her appearance from taking center stage. She coped with this by using self-deprecating humor and by minimizing the importance of looks. She used other assets—her warm heart, her generosity, and her strong work ethic—to put in balance the role beauty played in her life. We could see how heavily she relied on these other assets in ways that worked well most of the time, but held the potential of masking the work she needed to do on herself to enjoy her future as she aged.

We knew Jane felt proud of her very active involvement with the animals at the ASPCA and those she owned at home. There was endless need for her special talent, which allowed her to stay as busy as she was willing and able. She told us she also cared for her elderly parents, who lived nearby. *"My parents need a lot of help now and depend on their kids. I go over there after work as often as I can; and between them and the animals, I'm very busy."* We told Jane that we understood how these activities provided enormous satisfaction, but asked if it were possible that they also helped distract her from confronting her issues about aging. Jane readily agreed, saying, *"I hear myself complain about how much work I have, with all these people and animals who need me, but I also worry about what will happen when I won't be needed anymore. Or who will take care of me when I'm too old to care for myself? What will I do then?"*

Jane's life solutions clearly served to give her meaning and her work was important to those she cared for. But even Jane recognized she used her work to keep her from thinking about her future. We suggested that being so focused on others may have interfered with her ability to develop aspects of herself that could help her nurture other long-term pleasures, like her relationships with people outside her family and taking care of herself. We knew her appearance, or her lack of focus on it, was only one part of the equation that wasn't working toward a more optimistic future, but this is where our attention went. We felt this could change and Jane responded eagerly.

We asked Jane to recognize that dismissing the physical aspects of her life, which she had done all her life, was no longer as necessary as she thought. We told her that remaining far off the field, in fact, was likely contributing to the isolation she felt (and anticipated in her future). We believed that if she allowed her thoughts about her appearance to emerge more freely, and give the subject more value than she ordinarily did, she would open the window to other, deeper feelings about aging. Jane was game.

### Jane's Internal Dialogues: Opening Up to New Possibilities

As Jane shared her internal dialogues, we helped her hear the repeated theme of loneliness. Consistently, the words that emerged were about being alone and the dread of coping with increasing isolation as she aged. Our challenge was to get her to see the possibility that a part of herself that she'd largely written off—her appearance—could be a factor. *"I know my looks play a part in my pessimism, because I have so little confidence in ever attracting anyone. But having come from a large family, I really don't like the idea of having no one around. I'm so used to having company, noise, people and animals to take care of. I complained about there being too many of us when we were kids and now it feels scary to think that when my parents are gone and my animals get old, I'll be all by myself."* We told her that this could help her understand one of the reasons she felt so deeply attached to her animals. As she approached midlife and the end of her pets' lives, she was aware that the scenario was changing.

We suggested she talk out loud a bit more about why she felt so convinced that she would not attract anyone, why she assumed she was so unappealing, and that only four-legged creatures could love her unconditionally. *"When you put it that way, I realize it probably doesn't make sense to be so negative. Even ugly people meet people, get married, and have kids. Sometimes I'm astounded when I see attractive women marry ugly men. I usually think it's because the men have money. I rarely see attractive men with ugly women, but I guess you never know."*

We listened for possibility and hope as she continued talking, *"I just don't know if there's anything about me that would attract a man. If only a guy would give me a chance and get to know me. I feel I have something to offer, but nothing ever gets started. Or if it does, I just have such little confidence that it doesn't get past a first date."* We suggested that her lack of confidence was worth exploring. We were convinced that increased belief in her appeal, which meant letting go of an outdated sense of self, was key. We knew from other women whose stories were similar to Jane's that aging and maturity sometimes worked to give them a renewed sense of possibility. But first we had to take a look at the particulars of Jane's developmental history, to give us clues to her own personal path toward stepping onto the playing field.

## Jane's Family and History: Taunts That Linger

Jane wasn't born with the "plain" in her name. Clearly there must have been childhood influences that made her feel that way. We asked Jane to tell us something about her family background and especially her adolescence, which we felt were likely to explain how she came to identify herself as lacking in all things beautiful.

Jane was born into a large middle-class Irish family. *"There were five kids, all very close in age. I am the oldest. My dad made a good living, but I always felt we were short of money, what with five kids and my mom not working. My mom took care of us. We were a pretty ordinary, traditional family, with the women in the kitchen helping at home, and dad and my brothers sitting around doing guy things. My mom always catered to the boys. The last two kids my mom had were twins, born eight weeks premature. They were in the hospital for a long time and I don't think my mom ever really recovered. I was 12 when one of the babies died. She was just a couple of months old. Her twin, my little brother, is handicapped. It was awful, but we coped. As my dad always said, we put one foot in front of the other and keep going. That's the Irish for you."*

Jane described her family much the way she described herself, as having a no-nonsense approach to life that didn't allow for too much dwelling on what they didn't have. *"Being Catholic taught us to count our blessings. I don't think my family was really that different. Maybe we were closer than most. Helping each other was important. We went through some hard times, with my mother losing her baby, my youngest brother being sick a lot and my father drinking . . . did I tell you that? My dad drank a lot. He doesn't anymore, but that was after finally going to AA to get help. Now he's okay. We stuck together during it all."*

We wondered what it was like for Jane becoming an adolescent at the time her family was coping with the premature birth of the twins and the loss of her sister. *"There were bigger problems to deal with than teenage angst, but, as I said, my face was a mess. My acne was out of control and I just I didn't feel I could talk to anyone about it. Sure, I picked at my face. I've got some scars from that time. But it seemed like small stuff compared to what my mom was going through. My brother, being disabled, kept things in perspective. It's one thing to have bad skin and a lousy social life and another to be stuck in a wheelchair. My brother always had a great attitude. I didn't have much time for fooling around, so like my dad said, I put one foot in front of the other, helped out at home a lot and chugged along, like I do now."*

We confirmed Jane's perspective, that everyday problems seem small when surrounded by life-altering ones, but empathized with how hard it must have been to be a teen during traumatic times in her family. She continued, *"I remember thinking that I didn't want to grow up. It seemed like being an adult brought too many problems. My childhood was pretty happy, but so much changed when the babies were born. My dad's drinking was really bad for a while. He could get pretty abusive. But that's all in the past."*

As we listened to Jane's history, we could sense how she minimized her own emotional issues and needs in the service of providing comfort to the rest of her family. We also understood how getting older now, and watching her animals age, was reminiscent of the feelings she had about changes during her childhood and adolescence. We asked her to consider the possibility that she hadn't had the opportunity to focus on herself in important developmental ways, on some of the significant transitions of becoming a young adult. We reminded her that adolescent self-preoccupation and experimentation is taken for granted as part of growing up, in that it serves to help young girls grow into their adult and feminine identities. She believed she might have missed learning to care for her body and face during those important years while her mother was distracted by the family turmoil. And finally, we added that it was possible that her insecurity and inexperience in relationships now reflected the lack of opportunity to experiment socially and sexually during adolescence.

She confirmed this when she said, *"My relationships were mostly with my siblings and helping my mom. I wish I had the luxury of hanging out with friends and dating, but how does wish-*

*ing help? Besides, I really did have a thing about my face. At home, no one talked about it seriously, just kiddingly. My brothers had a nickname for me. They called me 'cheese face.' My mom tried to protect me. Our pediatrician told my mom he could put me on some medicine, but she didn't trust doctors, ever since her baby died. So, I had big zits and big boobs. Now I have sagging breasts and smaller zits. Wonderful.*" Her cynicism and resentment were coming through the more she talked.

We asked Jane if there was anything about herself she thought was attractive. She said, *"Well, no, not attractive, but I'm in pretty good shape. You have to be to take care of animals. I played soccer in high school. So I guess you could say my body doesn't have a lot of fat. I'm chunky, but muscular and strong."* We asked her too, if she were given the opportunity to enhance her appearance, would she? She said, *"Sure, especially if I could improve my skin. And maybe my hair. It doesn't go where I want it to."*

It was interesting that when given the chance to talk about her appearance, Jane became animated and involved, almost in spite of herself. It seemed that when her mask was lifted—the need to minimize what she couldn't value—a yearning to be more hopeful emerged. We asked her to consider the possibility that she might be able to let go of her apathy and hopelessness about ever meeting a man, if she worked on how she emotionally approached her appearance and relationships. We told her we were convinced that if she could enjoy herself more both physically and emotionally, she might be able to find someone who could join her in that experience. This required letting go and making a shift.

### Jane's Shift: About-Face Means Caring about the Face

More than the other women described above, Jane was most enthusiastic about making a shift in her attitude toward her looks. Perhaps this was because she felt as if she had little to lose, or because she felt so appreciative of the kind of attention she more often gave to others. In either case, Jane entered this process with eagerness.

First, we wanted Jane to understand how her looks had come to play the role they did in her life, in the context of her developmental history. We made clear again that she had *learned* to minimize, even dismiss, her appearance as she grew up, in part because of the physical issues that plagued her, but also because of the family dynamics that surrounded her. Jane's self-image reservoir had genetic vulnerabilities—like poor skin, uneven teeth—but external life circumstances led to more insecurity and discomfort about her looks. The extra attention, both emotionally and physically, that Jane needed from her caring family during adolescence wasn't available, leaving her reservoir with cracks and her self-esteem vulnerable for the rest of her life.

We helped Jane recognize that as a young girl, there had been little opportunity for her to manage her appearance in satisfying ways. We reminded her that this did not have to be the case now, since she had more choices. We felt she could use her uh-oh moment—the unhappy awareness that she wanted to, but couldn't, enjoy the holiday party at the ASPCA—and the memories it revived, to understand the circumstances that forced her toward isolation. Back in adolescence, she suffered humiliation around her bad skin, in private and alone. She felt guilty drawing family attention to what she believed was a struggle of relative unimportance. But now she could consider caring for her skin as she never had before, with some of the treatments available that could help her.

For Jane, uh-oh not only became ah-ha but oh my! She said, *"I never thought of my appearance in any positive way. I always thought, this is the way I am and the way I'll always be. But, maybe you're right, that I could do some things, now that I have my own money and the decisions are my own. Using my money doesn't take away stuff from my family, like it once did. I always felt that if I wanted to spend money on myself, like for a new pair of shoes, my mom would say there would be better use of money than spending it on frivolous stuff."* We encouraged Jane to begin thinking of caring for her face and body not as frivolous, but important, especially as she got older. Eating junk food as a teen was one thing. Now it was not only about feeding her body more nutritious food, but about making more informed choices that could be better for her health *and* her appearance.

With more discussion and some encouragement, we asked Jane if she thought she might be willing to emerge from her sheltered life with her animals. This required both letting go of her conviction that she was destined to be left behind, as well as giving herself the attention she needed to move forward. It meant seeing it less as a competition and more about joining other women in a similar challenge. Since we're all aging—beauty queens, valedictorians, wallflowers, and everyone between—Jane could see herself as more evenly placed. Although she felt she had lost time and had to learn some skills relating to people rather than her animals, she was eager to try.

Jane said she clearly wasn't headed to, nor interested in, radical changes in her appearance, but she did want to know what was out there that could possibly help her look better, especially regarding her skin. We mentioned that there were new treatments that helped acne at any age. We reminded her of the visit to the dermatologist she described, when the decisions were not her own. She said, *"It would be nice to have smoother skin, if it really was possible."* She asked about her hair next. We suggested that if she wanted to give it more volume, there were countless affordable products on the shelves and stylists willing to provide consultations.

As we talked more, Jane actually became tearful, thinking of all the years she had been unable to enjoy the possibility of taking some pleasure in her appearance. *"It makes me sad and maybe even a bit angry to think I could have avoided all that suffering. But there's no one to blame. It just would be great, not being embarrassed about my face and maybe even feeling confident when I see others looking at me."* We helped Jane keep perspective, that her lost time would have continued to be lost if she didn't make changes, but that there was no going back. People who try to undo what their past has brought them often unwittingly repeat it. Mourning what was, to make room for what can be, is the course we encouraged Jane to take.

Interestingly, the freedom to focus on her appearance in a positive way, led Jane to not only feel better, but actually to look more attractive. Instead of shame, she looked open and eager. Jane, at midlife, began to realize that aging in certain ways worked to her advantage. In comparison to other women whose looks have mattered a great deal, Jane felt far less competitive and jealous of others. She had the advantage of appreciating a newfound sense of pleasure in feeling more womanly, an experience she had never taken for granted.

At some point, Jane laughed, *"It's funny that I had to get to my 50s, when everyone is looking older, to realize that in some ways I was lucky that I never relied on my looks for anything. I have less to lose and maybe even more to gain."*

## Meet Vivian Diller, Ph.D.

Our scripts may be different, but the process is similar. Mine, like yours, can be broken down into six steps. Here is a description of how I became comfortable with my changing looks.

I am 56 years old, about 5'6", and in good physical health. I have a daughter, two sons, a stepson, and a two-year-old granddaughter. I live in Manhattan and work as a psychologist in an office that I share with my husband. He is a psychiatrist who specializes in couples therapy. My free time is spent mostly with family, friends, and involved in sports. I am an avid Yankees and Giants fan. I rarely miss a game on TV. I play tennis once a week, which helps me keep in shape. I recently took my first golf lesson in anticipation of needing to make that shift along with others as I age. Between family, work, sports, community service, and caring for my granddaughter once a week, I keep myself very active.

Like many women of my generation, I have had mixed feelings about how beauty fits into my identity. I grew up in a middle-class neighborhood and attended public elementary and high schools in Queens, New York. Both my mother and father were Holocaust survivors who maintained a strong connection to their Eastern European roots. They spoke Polish to each other and broken English to their children. Together they often reminisced about what they left behind—their homes, family, and friends. But they also celebrated their survival. They were deeply appreciative of the freedom they enjoyed in this country and the opportunity they were given to pursue the American dream. Patriotism, optimism, and giving back were key values held by my family, yet sadness and memories of the Holocaust were ever present.

My father was a doctor and my mother was his office manager and nurse. Their practice was on the first floor of our two-story home. I was one of three overachieving children. My older brother was the "prince," a good student and strong tennis player. He received his medical degree from Columbia and became a behavioral pediatrician. My younger sister was the "smart" one, the academic and musical child prodigy who played piano at Juilliard and earned scholarships to go to Harvard medical school. She became a psychiatrist. We were a very close-knit family but highly competitive. We held spelling bees (I always lost), trivia contests (lost those too), and ping-pong tournaments (I beat my brother once). I was a good student, athletic, and even somewhat musical but just not in the same league as my siblings. I was identified as the "pretty" one, a title that no one else really cared about. Although my dad had an appreciation for beautiful things, my mom managed the family finances and thought pretty clothes, makeup, and jewelry were unnecessary indulgences. I grew up as a tomboy who lived in hand-me-downs and who played stickball and ace-king-queen with my brother and his friends. It was only when my focus turned to ballet that my appearance began to matter to me.

My father introduced us to art and music. He sang opera as a young man and loved to perform for his family and friends. He nostalgically told us about his desire to become an opera singer and how sad it was when he had to give up his dream during the war. Music, he said, was forbidden while he was in hiding, since it meant risking being found by Nazis. My dad was the one who took me to my first ballet class. My parents were both very good ballroom dancers and they taught us the cha-cha, fox trot, and tango. They thought it was important for us to be graceful, even my brother, who was dragged to dance classes. I went eagerly. Ballet was breathtakingly beautiful, and I became gripped by a desire to become a ballerina. At age ten,

I was accepted into the Metropolitan Opera Ballet School and began spending all my afternoons and weekends at Lincoln Center in dance classes. As I entered adolescence, I focused more on ballet and less on school. After graduating from high school I made a decision—against my parents' wishes—to put my education on hold to pursue a dance career. Although they had supported my interest, driving me daily to and from classes and auditions, they were worried about the intense competition and difficult life I faced as a performer. But there was no stopping me. Ballet had become my life, and I went on to dance professionally for several years, during which time beauty became a large part of my identity.

I had some wonderful experiences as a ballet dancer and some very difficult ones. I was 16 when I began touring with a ballet company. I was young, lonely, and homesick. On the road a lot, I worked very hard, got little sleep, and felt exhausted all the time. I was given occasional solo roles but kept waiting for my big break. I tried harder and worked longer hours to reach every dancer's goal—a body that could show beauty with graceful perfection. But, as happens to performers who dance day after day on concrete stages, I got injured—shin splints, a torn hamstring, and an ankle break. Dancers are like athletes who wear tutus instead of protective gear. One injury, a career-ending metatarsal fracture, created chronic pain when I went on pointe. I knew at age 20 that my future as professional dancer had turned a corner and I was headed for a very tough time. On one hand, I felt lost without dance, which had consumed me for so long. On the other, I knew that I was facing an inevitable end to a short-lived career. I was confused, caught between trying to return to what I knew and moving forward toward my uncertain future. I decided to take some time off, go back to New York, and register for a couple of college courses.

A friend suggested that I try modeling to make some money while I figured out my life. I had a lot of time on my hands, going from being a dancer on tour to a "normal" college student. Like many ballet dancers, I looked like a teen in my 20s, and luckily the Wilhelmina Agency had a need for new faces in their junior department. I started modeling during the day and went to school at night. Although I felt fortunate to be making more money than I had ever made before, I didn't enjoy the work. I felt like a sham, flashing smiles when I wasn't happy, collecting payment for ads as the All American Teen, which clearly I was not. It was then that I realized I was continuing to hold on to a performance I didn't want a role in. I became determined to do something else and find a way to help other people navigate life transitions when their careers ended early. I decided to become a psychotherapist. I completed my undergraduate education and went on to receive a Ph.D. in clinical psychology and later a postdoctoral degree in psychoanalysis. Around that time I married my husband, who is a psychiatrist, and we started our family.

So, how did I experience the six steps toward dealing with changing looks? Well, clearly I had my first *uh-oh moment* long before many other women do, when I acknowledged in my 20s that I would never dance professionally again. It was a moment

VIVIAN DILLER

Height 5'6½"
Dress 5 - 6 - 7
Bust 32
Waist 22
Hips 34
Shoe 7½
Glove 6½
Hat 22
Hair Brown
Eyes Blue

*Wilhelmina*
9 EAST 37 STREET
NEW YORK CITY 10016

PRINT: 532-6800
TV: 532-7141

I will never forget, when I was faced with the fact that I wouldn't ever again move my body to music in ways that had given me so much pleasure. On the surface, this uh-oh moment may seem completely different than those confronted by women in midlife. But it was then that I began my journey, learning that letting go of youthful beauty can mean letting go of an aspect of self deeply embedded in identity. I didn't experience the same uh-oh feeling leaving modeling, which was more of a job than an identity. But I observed others struggling, as I did leaving dance, when they tried to find their footing after being forced out of their modeling careers. Leaving these careers, so based on youth and beauty, forced shifts in identity that I felt I wanted to write about in order to help others.

In retrospect, I realize that I too used *masks* to help me deal with the difficult feelings that came with making these transitions. I convinced myself that my appearance didn't matter and that intellectual pursuits did. By clinging to the values that my family had emphasized when I was growing up, I sought stability in a confusing time. I became determined to write the "perfect" dissertation in record time, much like I drove my body toward perfection when I danced. Not surprisingly, I wrote my thesis on the psychological difficulties inherent in choosing careers that are short lived. No longer able to rely on my looks to distinguish myself, I was now in search of other ways to find my identity. I didn't yet know what I had to leave behind, and that I had to allow mysef to mourn the loss.

My *internal dialogues*—the words I heard inside my head—in my 20s and even as I reached 50—revealed clues that helped me understand the role beauty played in my identity. I understood, for example, that I pursued ballet not only because I loved to dance but also because it brought beauty into the lives of my parents who had faced such ugliness during the war. On some level, I believed that the perfection associated with being a ballerina, and later as a model, offered a sense of control over my parents' chaotic past. For my mother, who had lost all of her hair, and my father, who had lost his teeth during the war, creating beauty provided a salve to their wounds. I knew, too, that I was reviving my father's dream, bringing music back into his life. I believed my success served as proof to them, and to me, that their struggles to survive had been worthwhile.

Looking back at my *family history and adolescence*, I learned that my reservoir had been based on a relatively firm and balanced foundation. Although my self-esteem had been narrowly focused on being the "pretty" ballerina, I realized that there were other aspects of my development that I could rely upon as I left dance behind. Adolescence had been about control over my body and emotional life. Young adulthood was about letting go, expanding how I defined myself, and finding a new balance after leaving dance. It was a shaky transition, but it was this difficult shift that motivated me to recognize the importance of developing a stable and broad sense of self to manage all of life's challenges.

I realize that when I gave up dance and modeling, the hardest part was *letting go*. As with the women described in this book, at midlife I had to understand the multiple meanings of my losses. Not only did I have to *mourn* the loss of my youthful physical self that had brought me professional success, but I had to let go of the role beauty held in my identity. I also had to mourn its role in my parents' lives, as I realized that the beauty brought into their current lives could not truly erase the horrific memories of their past. Trying to hold on to my youth-oriented careers kept me from moving on. It was a tough lesson, but I learned to shift my identity, once so focused on beauty, to the other aspects of myself that increasingly mattered to me.

In helping other professionals as they face aging out of their careers, I have found a satisfying way to use my previous focus on youthful beauty. Unlike dance and modeling, my career as a psychologist is one I will not age out of for a very long time. I feel great comfort knowing I can get better at what I do as I get older! I continue to work to care for my health and appearance and balance both with other aspects of my life. I see myself as a woman passing through midlife, aging as well as I possibly can. I am fortunate to have a husband and children who tell me they recognize changes on my face and body, but see them as expressions of my life experience. I truly believe I will always be beautiful to them and deeply appreciate that perception.

The six steps described in this book continue to be helpful to me with each passing year, with every change I see and feel. I know I will have to make ongoing shifts for the rest of my life—letting go, mourning, and moving on. I know I must continually redefine beauty as I age. With the eye of the beholder residing firmly within my own self, I am confident I can enjoy my aging appearance for the rest of my life.

Everyone ages, and as we do, we all meet on the same playing field. Not one of us can change the course of nature, but that doesn't mean our perspective on this natural process cannot change. We hope that the steps outlined in this book have helped shift uncertainty and confusion about your changing looks to feelings of acceptance and enjoyment, so that "looking as good as you feel" truly resonates with you for years to come.

# chapter ten

. . .

## Seeking a New Balance

*The most important thing about aging gracefully
is to not get old in your thinking.*

— Rebecca De Mornay

## Resolving the Beauty Paradox

You faced it! You are now at the end of our journey together.
A bit older, hopefully a bit wiser.

When you began, you were likely skeptical that two former
models, now psychologists, could offer useful ideas about your
aging looks. Whether you were hardly invested in your looks or
heavily focused on them, you probably also had little expectation that anything could help you *enjoy* your aging appearance.
Well, if we have taken the oxymoron out of that idea, then the
journey was worth your effort.

In addition to low expectations and skepticism, you probably approached the whole topic with ambivalence. You, along
with an entire generation of women, struggle with the cultural
dilemma we identified as the beauty paradox: looks matter, but
shouldn't; looks shouldn't matter, but do. Together, we first had
to reconcile our desire to look our best with our well-fought
right to be accepted and admired for other assets. You learned
that our process did not steer you away from these precious
privileges, but rather toward the right to *age* equally too.

We now recognize that getting older with grace and dignity requires the courage to acknowledge our current feelings and the maturity to mourn and move forward. You have read many stories about women seeking solutions amid ideological contradictions about aging and appearance. You discovered you were not alone feeling disequilibrium at this stage of life. Through our six steps, you found that resolution lies in a balanced relationship between your exterior self and your inner sense of self worth. Solutions were accomplished through internal work, by moving away from a self-image once rigidly attached to youthful beauty and replacing it with definitions that can continually be renewed. You learned that moving on meant becoming your age in a becoming way.

## Six Steps to Finally Facing It

We hope you will approach the six steps described in our book and summarized below with the kind of support and patience—and a bit of humor—that we all deserve at this phase in our lives. And remember, as you practice these internal steps toward external change, the goal is to feel *and* look beautiful for the rest of your life.

### Step One: Turn Your Uh-oh Moments into Ah-ha Ones!

The first step toward making any kind of change is acknowledgment. Decide if your concerns over aging and beauty are issues you would like to resolve. Take an honest, courageous look in your mirror and ask, *"Do you recall a moment in time that felt like a turning point in your aging process?"* Was there a moment when you said to yourself, *"I feel and look old"*? This first step allows you to own your honest feelings about your changing looks and see clearly through the paradoxical pulls that cloud your vision.

Through the stories of the women in this book, we see that uh-oh moments are experienced deep within us, as if something fundamental has changed in our identities. This is often accompanied by embarrassment and shame, as if we've been caught off guard and feel guilty that we care. We fear that we have lost control, as if abducted into an unwelcome phase of life. The first step is acknowledgment that our uh-oh moment exists and can be used to gain awareness. Only then can we turn uh-oh into ah-ha!

*Step Two: The Only Mask You Wear Should Be Made of Honey and Yogurt!*

This step is about coming out of hiding, from behind beliefs and actions that disconnect us from what we really feel. These behaviors make us look truly unnatural (those lips!), sometimes downright silly (those tight cutoffs!), and certainly distract us (those overtime hours!) from dealing with real issues. We are much better off removing the inappropriate cover-ups and allowing our vulnerability to show instead. Only then can we learn our genuine feelings. And they are often less problematic than the masks that cover them.

The reality is we *are* getting older, but aging doesn't have to be a dirty word. In other words, 40, 50, and 60 are just numbers, stages of life that don't have to—nor can they—be warded off. After all, what does 50 really look like today? It surely isn't the picture we have of our mothers or grandmothers. From our perspective, 50, 60, and older can look great if you take off your mask and let your face grow into becoming who you are. Masks are brittle. Masks are fake. Stop hiding. Take a look and see what's coming. You are getting older, but you're going to be more than okay.

*Step Three: Talk Back to Those Internal Dialogues*

Easy to say: face your uh-oh moment, take off your mask, and listen closely to the words you hear inside your head. Not so easy to do when the words you hear shout, *"You look old!"* We know, and hopefully you know by now that you're like millions of women who take a look at themselves and hear, *"You look tired. You look terrible. Give up. Give in. Get your face done, a little of this, a little of that. It's at least a fix. Fix what? You look like your mother. You're invisible. Too visible. Too old!"*

Maybe it's time we say "shush up" to the voices that get in our way. Listen to where these interfering voices originate. If you pay careful attention, you'll be able to hear that they most often come from your past. Sometimes they resonate with the voices we hear coming from the television or radio. Take hold of these dialogues and rewrite the script. You will always have conversations in your head. We all do, men and women alike. But you can create new lines, with new roles that speak to you in a kinder and gentler tone. The words come from your voice now. Speak up, loud and clear.

*Step Four: Give Mom Her Due. Take the Best of Her and Leave the Rest Behind.*

We all know that we tend to look to our mothers to explain why we are who we are—the good, the bad, and the ugly. But a lot of us are mothers now and know how easy it is to blame and be the recipients of blame rather than take responsibility and change. Sure, our mothers had an important influence on the development of our self-image, just as we do on the perception our children have of themselves. So did our dads, our siblings, and our teachers. *Vogue* and Revlon did as well! This step has taught us how that all developed.

We know that our mothers' role and all those other influences are reflected in a self-image that grew, stabilized, and became firmly rooted in our identities. That's why it is so hard to let go. But it's time to see these old reflections for what they are, take charge of them, and let them shift. Aging requires flexibility at any stage of life or we get stuck. The most reliable source of positive regard is reflected in the accommodating and accepting "I" of the beholder. And that is you!

### Step Five: Using Adolescent Memories Instead of Repeating Them

When we look back on adolescence, we can learn from the memories it evokes. Just a peek at your high school year-book picture may bring up feelings of awkwardness, uneasiness, volatility and instability. *"How weird I looked!"* Or, *"How strange I felt!"* Our self-criticism at that time is a close rival to the kind of harsh judgment we place on ourselves at midlife. The transitions during both phases are difficult, filled with confusing physical experiences, mixed cultural messages, and chaotic emotions.

As much as we may long for our youth, there's no way we want to be 15 again. We may long for the smooth skin, the energy, and the sense of possibility. Sure, those are the memories of adolescence we tend to nostalgically recall. But it might serve us well to also remember how we did—and did not—cope and use it to manage our feelings now. We have not gotten this far in life to get stuck feeling like teens in turmoil. Maybe this time around, we can avoid some of the impulsive, crazy decisions we made while feeling so topsy-turvy. Maybe we can get through these new transitions with fewer bumps and bruises, especially ones that are so hard to heal.

### Step Six: Saying Good-bye Is Hard to Do

We say good-bye to the "good ole days" and weep as we let go, much like we do all the losses in life. This loss is about detaching our sense of attractiveness from youth to make room for a broader, more flexible self-image. We can buy into the promises our culture offers to magically remove the changes we see on our faces and bodies. We can yearn to revive images of old selves and try to slow down the changes we see. Or we can accept reality. Aging does not stop. So, it's time to say good-bye, shed some tears, and then optimistically embrace our ever-evolving selves.

## Where You Are Now: Enjoying Your Looks at Any Age

As we conclude our journey together, let's remember with pride that we are a generation of women living much longer, extending the goalposts for what constitutes middle-age satisfaction and success. Although human nature leads us to desire longer lives, it is also natural to avoid the unknown, to yearn for what we do know, and cling to our youth. John Mayer sings, *"I'm scared of getting older. I'm only good at being young."* Well, to that we respond with strength and conviction, as Hillary Clinton did in her concession speech: *"Every moment wasted looking back keeps us from moving forward."*

It's time we all join together—as we approach midlife or beyond—and look confidently into the mirror on our walls *and* into our own more reliable internal ones. The gleam reflected back emanates now from our own eyes, seeing us as we really are. If we maintain this reflection, it will never fade. Let it mirror vitality, poise, hope, and wonder at what is next and be assured that this is what everyone else will see.

# appendix a:
# questionnaire

• • •

Use the following questions at
meetings, book clubs, or to stimulate
conversation over coffee!

1. What words do you use to define beauty?

2. Do you consider yourself attractive? Where would
   you place yourself on a scale of 1–10, with 10 being
   most attractive?

3. What is the first thought that comes to mind when
   you think of your looks changing with age?

4. What images does aging evoke? Describe the feelings
   associated with these images.

5. If you had to choose an age that most closely represents how you see yourself today, what age would
   that be?

6. At what age did you feel most beautiful? Is there a
   moment or image you have of yourself at that time?

7. How large a role would you say beauty plays in your
   identity and self-esteem? Please rate on a scale of
   1–10, with 10 being highest.

8. How does the culture of beauty impact you? Do you pay attention to what the media has to say about aging? A lot, a little, or not at all?

9. Describe your relationship with your mother. How has your relationship with your mother affected how you see yourself as a woman? How has it influenced your sense of beauty?

10. Describe your relationship with your father. How has your relationship with your father affected how you see yourself as a woman? How has it influenced your sense of beauty?

11. Do you see any parallels between your experience in adolescence and midlife? What was your definition of beauty as a teen?

12. If you have an adolescent daughter while you are in midlife, what is that like?

13. Do you feel competitive with other women in regard to beauty?

14. Did you experience envy during adolescence?

15. Do you see a relationship between your looks and your sexuality? Do you feel beauty plays a large role in your relationship with men?

16. Did you have a moment when you felt or thought, *"I'm no longer young."* When? What was that like?

17. How have you experienced menopause? What does it mean to you?

18. What would you say is the worst thing about aging and your changing looks?

19. What advice would you give to younger women as they face changes in their looks?

20. Which female public figure do you most admire for the way she is managing her changing looks? Why?

# appendix b:
# 12 tips for modern women

. . .

Sometimes we are asked how our six steps translate into practical ways to feel and look more attractive. Is it hypocritical to place emphasis on physical appearance at the end of a book that focuses attention on internal change? On the contrary. Our message involves caring about *both* our internal and external selves and recognizing the importance of how they interact. We've put together a list of tips that once were useful to us as models that we have found even more so now as our looks are changing. If you have worked the six steps and feel confident that beauty emanates from inside out, you will find them useful too. Unlike short-term beauty tips that instruct women on how to look young, these can be applied throughout life and are for all women.

### 1. Show Confidence and Pride Inside and Out
*Now that you know what it means to feel beautiful, project it! Feel it on the inside and show it on the outside.*
When we were modeling, we knew that models who walked into auditions with an air of confidence tended to get the jobs! It wasn't about being the prettiest—everyone was. Or about being perfect—no one was. It was about how you carried yourself into the casting room. Some models were known for their great legs, thick lashes, or long necks and used these assets to feel beautiful. Sometimes only a model's hands or feet were considered model material. Instead of focusing on features you

don't like about yourself, take the ones you do, embellish them and use them to contribute to your definition of beauty. Delicate wrists? Wear an eye-catching watch. Thick hair? An elegant headband or jeweled clip can bring just the right attention. Posture is a feature all women can enjoy if they keep their bones healthy. Women who walk with their backs straight and tall at any age exude pride and beauty. Hold your head up with poise and self-assurance and people will see what you feel.

## 2. Let a Radiant Smile Work for You
*Smiling goes a long way—from within . . . to your face . . . to others.*

There are models who are not perfectly shaped, nor model-thin or model-tall, who have successful careers because of their great smiles. Think of a baby's smile. Nothing brings more pleasure to the eyes of others than a baby's spontaneous toothless grin. Sure we might whiten, straighten, or bond our teeth, but regardless of how they look at any particular moment, smiling with warmth and a sparkle in our eyes goes a long way to convey beauty. Remember, beauty is not just in any one part of your body; not your face, your skin, your legs, or your breasts. Beauty is in the way you feel about yourself. It's in how you walk and talk and connect. It's in that joyful look on your face and in your eyes—no matter how many lines that smile brings along with it.

## 3. Reinvent Your Look
*With redefinition of beauty comes redefinition of style, attitude, and behavior.*

As models we had to constantly change our "look" for each and every job. It taught us to be flexible and capable of adjusting our appearance to the circumstances. You have learned how to let go of your rigid adherence to youthful looks and redefine beauty as you age. Instead of feeling anxious about change, have fun as you reinvent a look with each stage of life. Those tight jeans and short skirts might not work, but other styles may. Letting go of your former self-image doesn't mean neglecting your body and face. Keep in shape and adjust your routines according to your changing needs. Try walking instead of jogging. Yoga, in place of spin class. Play a set of doubles, rather than singles. Remember, it helps to be flexible, both physically and psychologically, so that your body can adjust to the changes in your looks.

### 4. Sexy at Sixty
*Sexy can feel and look beautiful. We're never too old for that!*
We have left behind our smooth faces, our tight skin and bright teeth, but we never have to leave behind our ability to connect to others sensually. That's what sexiness is about, a look that says, *"Connect to me, I am open and available."* As models we were sometimes told to "make love to the camera." With safety pins pulling at our clothes, fans blowing in our faces, sensual pleasure was not easy to feel, but we learned how to let our bodies and faces show it. And the more we let ourselves get into it, the more alluring we felt. Photographers often turn on sensual music to get models to feel "in the mood." A model can be absolutely exquisite, but her photos can look cold, sexless, and dull. It's not about the perfect body or the skimpy clothes she's wearing or not wearing. It's about the connection to the viewer that makes her appear sensual and beautiful. So it can be for you. The self-confidence you have gained in your changing looks, the openness you now feel to being adored is sexy at 60 or any age. Sexy can feel and look beautiful. Feeling beautiful can feel sexy.

### 5. Baseball Caps, Football Jerseys and Tees with Team Logos
*Start supporting your favorites! Wear gear that shows your passions—be it for politics, sports, music, or current events.*
A woman who has interests that go beyond age-defying remedies is one who conveys a vital approach to life. Sport the cap of your city's baseball or football team, or a T-shirt with a meaningful saying. Carry a recyclable "Save the Whales" or "Free Tibet" bag next time you shop for groceries. These

not only express your interests but also draw others in. Caps, T-shirts, and bags are the kinds ageless accessories. Try them on and see how you feel. You may actually end up having fun rooting for your team or supporting a new cause.

### 6. Work Out, Wax, Color, Manicure, and Go to Spas with Friends

*No more embarrassment about wanting to care for our faces and bodies. The secret is out, so let's enjoy the process together.*

Models are dressed, undressed, made up, and styled with other people coming and going all around them. Sometimes forced into uncomfortable situations (nothing like making quick outfit changes with 15 stage hands in full view!) at best we learned to laugh about it. Laughing with others made the work fun. Now that your desire to look good is out in the open, have fun. Do it with others. Take the tedium out. Instead of hiding your efforts, color your hair and pass the time chatting with a friend in the next chair. Or go to a salon where young women are getting highlights or coloring their hair blue. It's in style. Make it your style. Make dates to take care of yourself like you make plans to meet friends for coffee. Go to Weight Watchers as a group. Walk with weights in the park with a buddy. Use each other for support.

### 7. Take Advantage of Useful, Inexpensive Beauty Products

*Now that you are unafraid to see your face and body clearly, you will be better able to care for them.*

Try using a magnified mirror. It is an essential tool for models who inspect their faces for imperfections. You can use them now, not to scrutinize, but to help see! Most of us need glasses now, but wearing them while you apply makeup? These mirrors are like wearing glasses while you attend to your face. If uh-oh is now ah-ha you don't have to feel afraid to see the white hairs in your eyebrows or brown spots appearing here and there. You can pluck the white hairs if you don't want them, apply creams to the brown spots if you want them to fade, and apply makeup where it belongs. How many of us have left smudges of mascara above and below our eyes thinking they made it on to our lashes? Wouldn't it be great to blend your cheek color to avoid that clown-like look so often seen on women who don't take a careful look? By seeing yourself up close and personal, you can choose among the plethora of products available to adorn your beautiful self. Have fun!

## 8. Leave Competition Out of Beauty
*Looking and feeling attractive is no longer about holding onto or competing with youth. Envy and jealousy are never attractive!*
As models, competition was a necessary part of the work. We were constantly reminded that we could be replaced by a younger model who had a "new look." Rejection and competition was part of the process. It does not have to be now. To feel beautiful as you get older, try to look your best *for your age*, as healthy, robust, and vital as you possibly can. You are not in a race for the smoothest skin, the thinnest body, or the youngest-looking body. More importantly, looking good is not about a race with time. You know you'll lose that one. Let's get out of the competition we've imposed on ourselves and enjoy looking as well as we can. We'll all feel like winners.

## 9. Take the Plastic out of Plastic Surgery
*You don't have to look plastic if you decide to undergo dermatological or surgical procedures. Approach them thoughtfully with the right reasons.*
Once you stop trying hard to look young, younger, or even the youngest, make thoughtful choices to take advantage of what's out there to help you feel good about yourself. We're not *anti* anything, except panic, depression, and thoughtlessness about changing looks. If your inner eye feels comfortable with surgical procedures, just make sure you put yourself in the hands of trusted professionals who listen to what you want, not what they want. Don't feel pressured to make radical changes. Cosmetic surgery aimed at altering physical features so they

appear more in sync with your self image—like removing dark circles under your otherwise sparkling eyes—can surely bring increased pleasure. However, surgery performed with the hope of *changing* your self-image often leads to the opposite result. You are the one who will live with the alterations to your appearance, both the positive and the potential negative ones. How you look to yourself and others will be based on how you *experience* yourself, no matter what you do or don't do to your face and body. If your inner eyes feel you look attractive just the way you are, then so will the eyes around you.

### 10. Our New Movement Doesn't Need Infomercials
*Suggest reading* Face It *in your book club.*
No need to keep trying new products advertised on infomercials to defy your age. Defiance and fear are not pretty. Stop wasting your money, your time, and your face. Women *our* age can be beautiful for *our* age, and we can support one another. Let's join together to see ourselves as we are, living in our own skins that we wear with confidence and pride. Talk to other women and, as a group, let us work to affect change in the way we see ourselves as we age. We may even impact the way our culture experiences aging and beauty! Wouldn't that be worth the effort? Join the club. It's a lifetime membership!

### 11. Look Calmly Toward Your Future
*Now that you are less frightened of the anticipated changes in your looks, your face can exhibit the kind of calm that comes with facing fear head-on.*
There is nothing less beautiful than a face filled with terror. If you want to see unattractive faces, take a look at the ones in horror films. Unfurrow your brow, relax your face, and let that comfort show in a peaceful way as you move forward through the rest of your life.

**12. See Yourself as an Example for the Next Generation.**
*Do as I do. Our behavior is more important than the words we speak.*

At home, at work, and in social gatherings, you have the opportunity *and* responsibility to show younger women what beauty at midlife can be. Demonstrate the kind of poise and grace you want your daughters and younger colleagues to emulate. Remember, those who admire and respect you are the people you influence most. Let's provide the next generation with the kind of role models we weren't lucky enough to have. They deserve to look forward to midlife beauty, too!

# acknowledgments

. . .

The balancing act required to write this book—between a busy career, raising children, and an active family life—was challenging even for a former ballerina! I want to thank everyone who helped support me in completing *Face It*.

Thanks to John, my husband of 24 years, who not only inspires me intellectually but also tells me that I am, and will always be, the most beautiful woman in his life. I thank my children, Jordana, Gideon, and Gabe, my stepson, Seth, his wife, Jen, and my granddaughter, Sadie, for reminding me of what is most important in life; my in-laws Marcia, 92 and Arthur, 97, for being such exquisite models for aging gracefully; my sister, Emmeline, and my brother, Larry, for offering me constant sibling support, even while I rival their successes; my wonderful sister-in-laws, Heidi and Denise, for showing me what it means to be bright and beautiful at midlife; my dear friends Cindy, Marianna, and Marlene for convincing me that I can do anything and that anything I do will be successful. These relationships with family and friends reinforce the message in *Face It:* that the love you give and receive will show on your face and allow you to feel beautiful at any age.

A special thank you goes to Michele Willens for tirelessly transforming cumbersome psychological ideas into graceful words on the page. Not only is she a creative writer and talented editor but also a most loyal and generous friend. Without her, this book would not have been the enjoyable journey that it was.

Thanks to our agent, Jim Levine, who offered advice and encouragement from beginning to end. Although clearly not our target audience, Jim believed we had something important to say and made sure our message was clearly communicated. We are deeply grateful to Patty Gift and Laura Koch, our editors at Hay House, for making the process of publishing this book stimulating and pleasurable. *Face It* is the result of seamless team work between five strong-minded and supportive women who hope to inspire others to be the best—and most beautiful—they can be at midlife.

— Vivian Diller, Ph.D.

Jill also wants to thank her husband, Ed, for his patience, support, and insight, and her children, Matthew and Maggie, for their encouragement. Thanks also to Roger, Dale, and Rachel for their advice and assistance.

— Jill Muir Sukenick, Ph.D.

# endnotes

•  •  •

1.  Cowley, Geoffrey, "The Biology of Beauty," *Newsweek* 127 (1996): 60–67.

2.  Maestripieri, Dario, "Developmental and Evolutionary Aspects of Female Attraction to Babies," *Psychological Science Agenda* 18, no. 1 (January 2004), http://www.apa. org/science/psa/sb-maestripieri.html

3.  Aharon, Itzhak and Etcoff, Nancy et. al., "Beautiful Faces Have Variable Reward Value," *Neuron* 32, no. 3 (November 8, 2001): 537–551.

4.  Samuels, C.A. et. al., "Facial Aesthetics: Babies Prefer Attractiveness to Symmetry," *Perception* 23, no. 7 (1994): 823–831.

5.  Miller, Arthur G., "Role of Physical Attractiveness in Impression Formation," *Psychonomic Science* 19, no. 4 (1970): 241–243.

6.  Fox, Kate, "Mirror, Mirror," A Summary of Research Findings on Body Images, Social Issues Research Centre (1997), http://www.sirc.org/publik/mirror.html

7.  Nisbett, Richard E. and Wilson, Timothy DeCamp, "The Halo Effect: Evidence for Unconscious Alteration of Judgments," *Journal of Personality and Social Psychology* 35, no. 4 (1977): 250–256.

8.  Hoover, Gina and Arkkelin, Daniel, "Can't Buy Me Love: Effects of Masculinity, Femininity, Commitment, Attractiveness, and Income on Friendship, Dating, and Marriage Choices," Valparaiso University, Paper Presented

at the Annual Meeting of the Midwestern Psychological Association, Chicago (2002), http://faculty.valpo.edu/darkkeli/papers/mpa02/mpa02handout.htm

9. Etcoff, Nancy et al, "The Real Truth About Beauty: A Global Report, commissioned by Dove, a Unilever Beauty Brand (September 2004), http://www.campaignforreal-beauty.com/uploadedfiles/dove_white_paper_final.pdf

10. Life Expectancy Tables, http://www.efmoody.com/estate/lifeexpectancy.html.

11. American Society for Aesthetic Plastic Surgery (ASAPS), "Quick Facts: Highlights of the ASAPS 2008 Statistics on Cosmetic Surgery," http://www.surgery.org/download/2008QFacts.pdf

12. 12. Kally, Zina and Cumelia, Edward J. "100 Midlife Women with Eating Disorders: A Phenomenological Analysis of Etiology," *Journal of General Psychology* 135, no. 4 (October 2008): 359–377.

13. AARP, "Public Attitudes Toward Aging, Beauty, and Cosmetic Surgery," Research Report conducted by Roper Starch Worldwide Inc. (January 2001), http://assets.aarp.org/rgcenter/consume/cosmetic.pdf

14. Ibid.

15. ASPAS, "Quick Facts," http://www.surgery.org/download/2008QFacts.pdf

16. Fox, "Mirror, Mirror," http://www.sirc.org/publik/mirror.html

17. Etcoff, "The Real Truth About Beauty," http://www.campaignforrealbeauty.com/uploadedfiles/dove_white_paper_final.pdf

# about the authors

• • •

**Vivian Diller, Ph.D.**, is a psychologist in private practice in New York City. Dr. Diller was a professional ballet dancer before she became a professional model. She was represented by a top agency, Wilhelmina Models, appearing in *Glamour* magazine, *Seventeen* magazine, national print ads, and TV commercials. She left modeling in the late 1970s to begin her Ph.D. in clinical psychology at Albert Einstein College of Medicine, Yeshiva University. After completing her Ph.D., she went on to do post-doctoral training in psychoanalysis at NYU. As a psychologist, Diller works with individuals and couples, with a special interest in helping people transition out of youth-oriented careers. Dr. Diller wrote her doctoral dissertation on the psychological profile of the professional dancer. Her dissertation has served as a model for character studies at Ph.D. programs in psychology around the country. She has written subsequent articles on related topics and has been consulted for pieces written by others on beauty, aging, eating disorders, models, and dancers. She has served as a consultant to a major cosmetic company interested in promoting age-related beauty products, and has made numerous appearances on television discussing issues about beauty and aging. Vivian lives with her husband, John Jacobs, M.D. and their three children.

Websites: **www.VivianDiller.com**
**www.FaceIttheBook.com**

**Jill Muir-Sukenick, Ph.D.**, is a psychoanalytic psychotherapist in private practice in New York City. Dr. Muir-Sukenick was signed with the world's top modeling agency, Ford, and modeled professionally throughout the 1970s and '80s. By the late '80s, Dr. Muir-Sukenick made the transition from modeling to acting, performing on television and in films. Following that, she pursued an academic career, getting her Ph.D. from NYU in clinical social work. She wrote her dissertation on narcissism and self-esteem in adolescent female models and the role of perceived parental narcissism. In addition to having a private practice, she continues to be active in the modeling world as a counselor to models and a consultant to modeling agencies. Her interest in the ways in which models experience aging grew out of earlier studies she conducted with Dr. Diller concerning how models made the transition from their profession into other arenas. Muir-Sukenick is often interviewed by the media for her special expertise on beauty. She has served as a consultant to a major cosmetic company interested in promoting age-related beauty products, and has made numerous appearances on television discussing issues about beauty and aging. Jill lives with her husband, Ed Sukenick and their two children.

Website: **www.JillMuirSukenick.com**

**Michele Willens** has been a longtime journalist, with articles in the *New York Times, Los Angeles Times, McCalls,* and others. She is also a playwright: her works include *Dear Maude, Don't Blame Me, I Voted For Helen Gahagan Douglas* (co-writer) and *Family Dinner.* She is chair of the board of City Lights Youth Theatre and resides in New York City with her husband, *Dateline* Executive Producer David Corvo, and their two children.

# Hay House Titles of Related Interest

*YOU CAN HEAL YOUR LIFE, the movie,*
starring Louise L. Hay & Friends
(available as a 1-DVD program and an expanded 2-DVD set)
Watch the trailer at: **www.LouiseHayMovie.com**

*THE SHIFT, the movie,*
starring Dr. Wayne W. Dyer
(available as a 1-DVD program and an expanded 2-DVD set)
Watch the trailer at: **www.DyerMovie.com**

• • •

*THE AGE OF MIRACLES: Embracing the New Midlife,*
by Marianne Williamson

*JUICY LIVING, JUICY AGING: Kick Up Your Heels Before
You're Too Short to Wear Them,* by Loretta LaRoche

*THE SECRET PLEASURES OF MENOPAUSE,*
by Christiane Northrup, M.D.

*WHAT IS YOUR SELF-WORTH?: A Woman's Guide
to Validation,* by Cheryl Saban, Ph.D.

All of the above are available at your local bookstore,
or may be ordered by contacting Hay House (see next page).

• • •

We hope you enjoyed this Hay House book.
If you'd like to receive our online catalog featuring
additional information on Hay House books and products,
or if you'd like to find out more about the Hay
Foundation, please contact:

Hay House, Inc., P.O. Box 5100, Carlsbad, CA 92018-5100

**(760) 431-7695** or **(800) 654-5126**
**(760) 431-6948 (fax)** or **(800) 650-5115 (fax)**
**www.hayhouse.com®** • **www.hayfoundation.org**

• • •

*Published and distributed in Australia by:* Hay House Australia Pty.
Ltd., 18/36 Ralph St., Alexandria NSW 2015 • *Phone:* 612-9669-4299
• *Fax:* 612-9669-4144 • www.hayhouse.com.au

*Published and distributed in the United Kingdom by:*
Hay House UK, Ltd., 292B Kensal Rd., London W10 5BE • *Phone:*
44-20-8962-1230 • *Fax:* 44-20-8962-1239 • www.hayhouse.co.uk

*Published and distributed in the Republic of South Africa by:*
Hay House SA (Pty), Ltd., P.O. Box 990, Witkoppen 2068 • *Phone/Fax:*
27-11-467-8904 • info@hayhouse.co.za • www.hayhouse.co.za

*Published in India by:* Hay House Publishers India, Muskaan
Complex, Plot No. 3, B-2, Vasant Kunj, New Delhi 110 070 • *Phone:*
91-11-4176-1620 • *Fax:* 91-11-4176-1630 • www.hayhouse.co.in

*Distributed in Canada by:* Raincoast, 9050 Shaughnessy St.,
Vancouver, B.C. V6P 6E5 • *Phone:* (604) 323-7100 •
*Fax:* (604) 323-2600 • www.raincoast.com

## Take Your Soul on a Vacation

Visit **www.HealYourLife.com®** to regroup, recharge, and recon-
nect with your own magnificence.Featuring blogs, mind-body-spirit
news, and life-changing wisdom from Louise Hay and friends.

Visit **www.HealYourLife.com** today!